THE RIGHT WINE WITH THE
RIGHT FOOD

THE RIGHT WINE WITH THE RIGHT FOOD

Jeffrey Benson and Stuart Walton

RIGHT WAY

Typeset in 11pt Times by Letterpart Ltd., Reigate, Surrey.

Printed and bound in Great Britain by Cox & Wyman Ltd., Reading, Berkshire.

The *Right Way* series is published by Elliot Right Way Books, Brighton Road, Lower Kingswood, Tadworth, Surrey, KT20 6TD, U.K. For information about our company and the other books we publish, please visit our website at www.right-way.co.uk

CONTENTS

INTRODUCTION

For some people, the business of finding the right wine to go with a particular dish is something approaching an exact science. As with any scientific discipline, they feel, it must have its founding principles and its eternal laws, and the slightest intrusion of human error can result in just as much of a calamity as a civil engineer's slip with a protractor might do with a suspension bridge. We would like to make it clear here and now that we do not belong to this school of thought.

It is certainly true that there are food and wine combinations that simply don't work, for example where too strong a wine overpowers the flavour of a dish, or vice versa. Partnering a high-acid dry white wine with a richly creamy dessert will produce tears before bedtime, and if you have laboured all afternoon over a recipe that involves fine ingredients and a complex and enticing range of flavours, it would be rather letting the side down to serve a very basic *vin de table* with it. The exercise of sheer common sense, more than the mobilisation of any in-depth wine knowledge, is enough of a guide in these cases. What seems to have happened in recent years, however (led by the most punctilious authorities in viticultural Europe, namely the French, but followed enthusiastically since by the Americans and lately the British), has been a shift towards a much more finely detailed approach to the subject. It is possible to attend food-and-wine matching classes in one's spare time, some of them – as in California – organised by the winemakers themselves, others offered as evening courses at the local adult education centre.

Perhaps this isn't an entirely new phenomenon after all. One of us had the profoundly instructive experience in the 1960s of finding himself seated next to an eminent eye surgeon at a smart New York dinner party. As though the world of opthalmology were not demanding enough, this gentleman had managed to find time to pursue a sideline in gastronomic studies with singular fervour. He was of confirmed opinions as to which wine made the perfect fit with practically any classic dish, but one match had for many years continued to elude him. What was the best wine to drink with spaghetti bolognese?

Although it may not seem like the most difficult of dishes to please, nothing had quite met with the doctor's unqualified approval. Oh, there were wines that just about worked if you were prepared not to think about it too closely, but then he did think about it closely. The problem all but kept him awake at nights until one day, in the kind of sweet serendipity with which the history of scientific investigation is strewn, revelation happily dawned. There was only one wine ultimately – just as he knew there would be – that properly went with spaghetti bolognese. And it wasn't an Italian wine, as one might have expected, given the provenance of the dish. It was Château Lafite, a *premier cru* claret from the Médoc district of Bordeaux. Not even any old Lafite either, but specifically the 1953 vintage.

The triumphant medic was in deadly earnest, and was able to justify his conclusions with impeccable logic. And it has to be admitted that, had the occasion arisen to put them to the test, not many of us would turn down the chance of drinking a top Bordeaux in a fine vintage as against the corner-store Chianti we might otherwise be faced with. The point, of course, is that one can go too far. Anybody tempted to try out the combination today should bear in mind that the '53 Lafite will taste rather different now from how it tasted in the 1960s, and so it isn't even as if the finding will stand us in good stead for all time.

It is precisely this sort of manic precision that alienates those who have neither the inclination nor the budget to go into the subject in such detail, and readers may be relieved to hear that Château Lafite is not one of our suggestions to drink with spaghetti bolognese. That said, there has since been something of a backlash against this type of approach, in the course of which it has got about that there isn't really any point at all in worrying, in some arcane technical sense, about whether a particular combination of food and wine actually 'works' or not. Just choose a wine you like, and get on with it. This sounds beguiling enough – refreshingly free of snobbery, you might think – but it can lead, as suggested above, to pairings that spoil the enjoyment of either the food or the wine or both. What would be the point of drinking a powerful red Australian Shiraz with a starter of lightly grilled scallops, and a delicate, youthful Muscadet with casseroled beef, when the pairings would so obviously work better the other way around?

In this book we aren't out to tell you what you should and shouldn't drink. Even today, when a lot of the snootiness has been removed from the topic of wine, and wine consumption is on a seemingly unstoppable upward curve in all sectors of society, people can still be far too shy about expressing preferences and stating opinions when it comes to wine. There is still an inbuilt fear of 'getting it wrong'. We shall do our best in these pages to dispel any lingering mystique about the subject by means of helpful and unpatronising suggestion, as opposed to dogmatic elitism. Our aim is to give as wide a spectrum as possible of advice on what to drink with what, often recommending wines that are quite stylistically distinct from each other with the same food, in the hope that you may be emboldened to try different combinations as the occasions arise and see which ones suit you best. And rather than simply listing our suggestions in shorthand fashion, so that you have to take them on trust, we have tried where appropriate to give reasons for our advice, explaining the gastronomic logic behind them. We don't always agree with each other in these matters, so we would hardly expect to convince everybody who uses this book to arrive at the same conclusions.

In the dim, distant past, the basic rules of choosing wine with food amounted to little more than drinking dry white wine with fish and red wine with meats. If you wanted a drink beforehand, you had a sherry or a gin and tonic, and if you wanted something at the end of the meal, you had a brandy or a liqueur. There was champagne for special occasions, and dessert wines for – well, desserts. And that was about it. What *type* of dry white wine went with the Dover sole, or red with the roast beef, didn't really much matter in an era when there was a far narrower range of wine to be had than there is these days. Most of it, in any case, was French, with the other main western European countries (Italy, Germany, Spain and Portugal) putting in only sporadic appearances for curiosity value. It should be recalled that an unfortified table wine from Portugal was once as unusual a commodity on the wine-merchant's shelf as the likes of Uruguayan, Moroccan or Mexican wines now are.

Eventually, by about the 1970s, these apparently

hard-and-fast rules got a little altered in the wash, so that it became permissible to drink a dry white wine with a white meat such as pork or poultry, while reserving the red wines for the darker meats like beef and lamb. The method of cooking turned out to make a difference. A poached chicken breast with a light creamy sauce was better served by a white wine, but a whole roast chicken seemed somehow to be done more obvious justice by a light to midweight red. There were even reports of some adventurous souls – avant-garde mavericks, clearly – who had been known to drink light red wines with certain fish dishes.

What has happened since then, broadly speaking, is that just as the array of available wines has expanded, so too has the range of types of food we eat. Classic French and Italian dishes have now been joined by Far Eastern cuisines such as those of Thailand and Japan. There are Lebanese restaurants on the high street, jostling cheek by jowl with Mexican and Greek, with the odd Vietnamese or Turkish interloper peering out from among them. And even before the appearance of these newcomers, at least in the UK, there were the old standbys of Indian and Chinese food that added a note of the exotic and the far-flung to the home-grown and traditional European dishes with which people were most familiar. (The difference was that nobody expected to drink wine with red-hot curries and sweet-and-sour pork, whereas now we are ready to drink wine with almost anything.)

So cosmopolitan have tastes in food become that, led by the urban restaurant scene, a fashion for picking and mixing different national styles within the same menu, even within the same dish, has arisen. This has undermined at a stroke one other eternal verity of food-and-wine matching: if in doubt, match a traditional dish from one of the wine-producing countries with one of that country's wines.

If you are about to set to with a salad of chicken, chorizo sausage and pasta quills dressed with chilli-spiked crème fraîche, you might be forgiven, when contemplating the wine list, for losing your bearings a little.

We have tried to afford the reader a safe passage through the obstacle course represented by the eclectic approach to cooking, despite its evident complexities, as well as through the more closely charted terrain of classic national cooking styles. What we have borne in mind throughout is that, while a book like this is only useful if it acknowledges the flexibility that the global larder (and the global wine cellar) now demand, there is equally no point in going for the confusingly non-committal, completely *laissez-faire* approach. We are always open to new suggestions, but not so open-minded as to entertain any old bit of nonsense. Drinking a dry sparkling wine with a dessert – still an article of faith in parts of France – is not the kind of suggestion to cut much ice with us, and we don't mind telling the French as much when faced with such a grating clash of flavours. Neither do we forget, though, that taste is an intensely personal matter, and that while for some it may suddenly seem the last word in sophistication to drink a lightly textured red, such as a New Zealand Pinot Noir, with grilled salmon, to others the combination seems a clumsy one. One of us can't bear the partnership of red port and Stilton, but isn't about to tell generations of readers for whom it is one of the highlights of a gastronomic Christmas that they don't know what they are doing.

Eating and drinking well are among life's most cherishable treasures. If we make them the subject of a pontificating scholastic exercise, such as our opthalmologist friend had done, then in one very real sense we are taking something of that pleasure away from them. It is often observed that people who taste wine for a living, such as those who work in the wine trade and those who write about the subject, lose something of the ability to enjoy wine in an honest-to-goodness, uncomplicated, non-technical way because we are always analysing and evaluating it. Spending a good portion of one's life trying to find the right gustatory soulmate for spaghetti bolognese similarly risks stripping much innocent enjoyment from the business of eating.

The fact remains, though, that there are good food and wine matches, and then there are occasionally those that seem to reach perfection because every aspect of the combination – from aroma to texture to flavour to the mingled aftertaste of the two elements – seems to be in harmonious balance with every other. No book can ensure that you will always find such perfection in your matches, since there are so many variables at work. (The French have it right when they say that there are no good wines *per se*, only good *bottles* of wine. Each one is different, just as each time you cook the same dish, it will turn out slightly differently from the last time you made it, for any number of reasons.) We are against drab standardisation in winemaking, and so we have no wish to introduce it into the matter at hand. What we can and shall do in these pages is offer some pointers to maximise the likelihood of finding one of those ideal marriages of solids and liquids, or at the very least of enjoying both of them together more than they would otherwise be enjoyed singly.

Bon appétit, then, and keep experimenting. Pleasant surprises make life worth living, and this subject is teeming with them.

1

SERVING

The ways of ruining a perfectly good dinner are as number-less as the stars. Many of them have to do with the manifestation of cigarette smoke at critical moments. The loud declaiming of idiotic opinions is always a winner, while some people time the announcement of major dietary restrictions to a nicety, wrong-footing the hosts as their coats are taken on arrival: 'By the way, my numerolo-gist won't let me eat any food that has more than five letters in its name. I hope that isn't going to be a problem.' Contributing a bottle of wine to the proceedings is a universally appreciated gesture, but arriving with a tissue-wrapped bottle of unchilled retsina and cheerily bellowing 'Right, let's get the party started!' may be over-egging the convivial pudding.

Serving wines that are inappropriate with the dishes is another sure-fire way to spoil the occasion, and the *raison d'être* of this book is to help you avoid such a calamity. However, before we get down to the main business of matching food and wine, it is as well to be aware of some of the basic technical matters surrounding the actual serving of wine. We have, depending on the occasion, found ourselves drinking wine from china mugs, polysty-rene cups, half-pint glasses in pubs, and those clear plastic receptacles they hand out on Economy Class flights that can split and shred the lips. But while there is such a thing as making a virtue of necessity, there is still no likelihood of producing a silk purse from a sow's ear. In short, some ways of doing things work better than others, and it doesn't have to be a matter of snobbery or exclusivity to point this out. A white wine at room temperature is like a snowdrop in July, while a tot of pale dry sherry served from a bottle that was opened at the coronation of George V does nothing either to whet the appetite or raise the spirits.

Here, then, are the main points to be aware of when looking to enjoy wine in its best (that is, gastronomic) context.

Glassware

It is just conceivable that the proverbial lady's slipper is the best receptacle of all from which to drink a good wine (we couldn't possibly comment), but those plastic cups and half-pint glasses mentioned above most certainly will not do. The point of good glassware is not that it be expensive or exquisitely decorative; it is that it should be the right shape and size.

As a general rule, when buying new wine glasses, choose those that have long stems and wide bowls, and that taper towards the rim – in other words, that are tulip-shaped. A major part of enjoying wine lies in appreciating its aroma. This doesn't mean you have to go through the whole wine-taster's performance of swirling and sniffing before every mouthful, but a momentary registering of what was once quaintly known as its 'bouquet' certainly enhances the sense of anticipation prior to tasting it. A glass that funnels those scents towards the nostrils is obviously more efficient in the matter than one that casts the bouquet into the air like the bridal posy at a wedding. This latter effect

Burgundy   Bordeaux   White wine

Port   Champagne

is what a flared glass inevitably produces. Avoid trumpets. Think tulips.

A wine glass should always be of a decent size. Not only does it remind us that wine is not yet (*pace* the medical fraternity) subject to public rationing, it also helps crucially in the enjoyment of those aromas by allowing the drinker to swirl the contents gently. To this end, the glass should never be filled more than about a third full. The alternative is a glass that is so small it *has* to be filled up, on pain of appearing unbearably parsimonious. These standard small round wine glasses, the polite term for which is 'Paris goblets', are the ones still widely used for wine in pubs and old-fashioned bistros. If you have a set, start being a little careless with them when drying them or hurling them towards the dishwasher, so that by natural wastage, you will soon have the perfect pretext to buy some new ones. Broadly speaking, a white wine glass should hold about 20cl/7 fl oz and a red wine glass about 35cl/12 fl oz.

Led by an internationally renowned Austrian glass firm called Riedel, some manufacturers now make different designs of glass for different wines – and not just red, white and sparkling. There is a glass for each different grape variety, one for non-vintage champagne and one for vintage and so forth. Believe it or not, they do seem to work in delivering a more multi-dimensional appreciation of each respective wine, but finding the shelf-space to accommodate a full set of each one of them might present a challenge. All you really need is one set for white, one larger set for red and a set of flute glasses for anything with bubbles. If you feel two sets are quite enough to be going on with, buy the flutes and the larger specimen of the other kind, and use the latter for both white and red.

Plain glass is much better than coloured or patterned. Tinted glass obscures the colour of the wine; a dark glass makes red wines look unsettlingly muddy. The postwar vogue for sets of glasses in which each was a different colour may have looked racy enough at the time (at least until petrol stations started giving them away), but they are best kept for water now. Cut crystal can look very attractive, but it still detracts from the uncomplicated appreciation of a wine's appearance. Keep the drinking vessel as neutral as can be, and the liquid poured into it will be all the more radiantly highlighted. And the thinner the glass from which it is made, the better it is.

Look after your glasses too. Wash them by hand in good hot water, and let them have pole position at the washing-up. The sticky plates and encrusted roasting dish can wait.

Dry them gently with a soft glass cloth, so that they are sparkling clean for the next use.

Table-setting

When laying the table for an occasion at which a number of different wines will be served, place the glasses at the top right corner of each setting, with the glass for the first wine nearest to hand. If you are having three wines, it may be as well to cluster them so that the second and third stand closely behind the first, like bodyguards around a teenage pop sensation. You ought really to have a tall, straight-sided glass for water as well, and be sure to advise guests – while taking care to sound as little like a Scout leader as possible – which glass is for which liquid. That way, all potentially discomfiting uncertainty is banished.

Serving Temperatures

It must be remembered that modern-day serving temperatures for wine bear very little relation to those that obtained in the great houses with their private cellars in the nineteenth and early twentieth centuries. To keep warm in the withdrawing-room involved bagging a place near the open coal fire in the grate, protected from the worst of its glare by a screen, and not stirring from it until it was time for retiring. Wines brought up from the cellar in the winter months might well have been in an advanced state of frostbite, with the condition known as 'room temperature' something more like what we would regard as chilled.

Despite the absence of cellars in modern homes, these were not necessarily poor guidelines. Much red wine is drunk in too warm a condition, particularly in the summer months, a tendency much exacerbated by the habit of some retailers of designing shops in which strong spotlights are focused on the bottles, subjecting the wines within to a continuous slow cookery, as gentle but indomitable as that which one would accord a meringue. By the same ham-fisted token, much white wine is served too cold, an indignity that strips from it all the characteristics of refinement it possesses and renders the drinker's palate similarly insensate. Emergency recourses in these circumstances are not of the most delicate: a warm red wine can be given a half-hour in the fridge, if time allows, but an over-chilled white wine must be left, shocked and shivering to its marrow, to come round of its own accord. Warming the glass by cupping it solicitously in both hands, like a carol-singer with a wassail bowl, gives it a fighting chance of recovery. (One of us, invited to give a public tasting at the Ideal Home Exhibition, was once confronted immediately before the show by a batch of white wines that had been left overnight in a refrigerator cold enough to have preserved body tissue. They had largely frozen, and internal expansion in the bottles had led them to begin forcing out their corks. As the first of an eager public who had paid ready money for the occasion came pouring through the door, they were treated to the indescribable spectacle of a so-called 'wine expert' dunking and twizzling bottles by the pair in a bucket of steaming-hot water.)

As a rough guide, common-or-garden sparkling wines and the very sweetest white wines, such as Sauternes, can be served at the chilliest temperatures: about 5-6°C/41-43°F. The majority of dry white wines, good champagne, rosés and the drier styles of sherry (fino and manzanilla) should come to the table somewhat less cold: 9-10°C/48-50°F. Some light red wines, such as most Beaujolais (though not its weightiest example, Moulin-à-Vent), northern Italian and any of the rare German reds, benefit from being served very slightly chilled to emphasise their freshness: 12-13°C/54-55°F. Most other reds and the darker, sweeter styles of fortified wine can be served at room temperature, although note that that should not ideally exceed 15-16°C/59-60°F. If you like your central heating considerably higher than that, your reds will suffer, and your whites – however painstakingly chilled beforehand – will warm up too quickly unless the bottle is kept in an ice-bucket.

Serving Order

In an ideal world, such as this is not, the order of service for a multi-wine occasion would proceed in stately progress from a dry aperitif such as fino sherry or brut champagne, to a dry white with a first course, fish or seafood dish, to a red to accompany the main-course meat, and finally subside into a tot of one of the richer fortified wines, such as port or madeira, with the cheeses. Naturally, not every dinner will conform to this classic pattern. There are those menus where a meaty starter dish is succeeded by a main course of white fish, or where a savoury dish deemed worthy of a sweet wine accompaniment (such as a rich, livery pâté) is followed by a dish that naturally mandates a dry wine. Such a proceeding is by no means wrong, but it needs strategic pauses between courses to enable guests to finish the remainder of the first wine before the next is embarked on, and here you will find that ice-cold mineral water is a particular boon, to refresh the palate and neutralise the flavour of the last wine in time for the appearance of its successor. Sometimes, there may be no place at all for a red until the cheese stage, in which case a light, herbaceous dry white without oak should be followed by a richer, creamier, cask-aged creation.

A further general rule is to run from relatively ordinary

wines up to any more illustrious bottle, creating the impression of a steady ascent to the summit, as opposed to a rolling downhill in neutral. Your bargain-priced Hungarian Sauvignon Blanc (a perfectly good wine in itself) will not be flattered by appearing in the wake of a hang-the-expense bottle of Meursault. 'The only enemy of a good wine,' they say in Portugal, 'is a better one.'

Serving Sparkling Wines

Everybody knows how to open a bottle of sparkling wine, surely. You give the bottle a good shake, as though you were making Margaritas for a graduation party, you tear the foil, the wire cage and the cork away as quickly as you can, producing the kind of explosion that gives household pets a heart attack, and then direct the spurting jet of fizz into the faces of the assembled company, so that all and sundry are happily doused in the stuff, and will be sent away laughing all the way to the dry-cleaner's. If there is any left in the bottle, you put it to your lips and swig the remainder down with a look of triumph.

That at least is the correct method for the Formula One racing drivers among you. For the rest, a rather more circumspect approach is called for. Making the cork go pop is really not the point of opening sparkling wine. It should be gently eased free with the merest sigh. To this end, it is as well to ensure the bottle has not been rudely agitated in the days leading up to its being broached, and that it is properly chilled. A colder bottle will be less likely to erupt than one that has only just seen the fridge. Once the foil and wire have been removed, the best technique is to turn the cork one way and the bottle the other simultaneously (easier than it sounds), controlling the release of the cork with a thumb over the top as soon as you feel it beginning to give. Have the glasses near to hand, so that if there is any unexpected overflow from the bottle, you can direct it towards the nearest one. Some feel a little more secure if the whole operation is performed with a tea-towel or glass cloth in one hand, but it shouldn't be strictly necessary.

The number one rule, despite the antics at Silverstone, is never to point the unopened bottle towards anybody. A flying cork can cause serious injury. What you want is a delighted 'Whoopee!' from your guests, not massed gasps of horror.

Leaving Red Wines to Breathe

Should you or shouldn't you? The younger the wine, the more it will benefit from being poured out into a jug or decanter and left for at least half an hour (an hour even better) to get some air. Aeration helps to soften up the tannin in young red wines, making them altogether more agreeable to drink. In the case of older vintages, a short period of air contact (15 minutes or so) will allow what the trade picturesquely refers to as 'bottle stink' to blow away. Spanish wines labelled 'Reserva' shouldn't theoretically need to breathe. They have been cask-aged by the winemaker, and are intended to be in a drinkable condition as soon as the bottle is opened.

White wines need no breathing time. It is very important, however, if you decide to aerate a red wine, to pour it out into another container. The practice often seen of simply taking out the cork and leaving it makes virtually no difference to the wine, as only a tiny surface area at the top of the bottle is in contact with the air. If you haven't got anything suitable for bringing to the dinner-table, pour the wine into something like a measuring-jug out of sight of your guests, and then funnel it back into its original bottle. Even this simple act makes a considerable difference to its texture. After that, most of its development will take place as it sits in the glass, so don't be in too much of a hurry to knock it back.

Jugs, Decanters and Buckets

Should you feel that bringing a bottle to the table is a touch *infra dig*, there is a range of alternative receptacles in which wine may be served. Older wines may need decanting to separate them from their sediment (for which process, see below), and for this only a decanter will do. Like the wine glasses themselves, a decanter should be of plain glass, and come with a stopper. It need only be relatively small and of a design that blends in with the rest of the tableware. There was a passing fashion in the 1980s for ship's decanters, the kind that has a disproportionately wide base to prevent it from overturning as your vessel lists to starboard, or something of the sort. Unless you fear that you might be embroiled in naval manoeuvres *very* often, there is no need for this. They anyway handle in a most ungainly fashion.

For everyday reds that are too young to have thrown a sediment, a simple glass jug will do. There is a particular kind of British design called a claret jug, an elegantly tall pitcher with a handle on the side and a wide spout, but no stopper. This is a good, versatile container in which to allow such wines to breathe, and will prove a worthwhile investment.

White wines and sparklers may be served in an ice bucket for that extra touch of pizzazz. Not to be confused with an ice-container, which has a lid and a pair of tongs and is for keeping ice in at a cocktail evening, the ice bucket looks more like an actual bucket, has handles on each side, no lid and is intended to be filled with not just ice, but with a mixture of ice and water. An unchilled bottle will cool down pretty rapidly given this treatment, and if anything, you need to be careful not to overdo it. If the bottle seems to be getting too agonisingly cold, then take it out of the bucket. A dish-towel or other cloth is essential for serving from an ice bucket, as the bottle will otherwise leave a trail of icy drips across the table as the wine is poured.

Decanting

Red wines that are more than around eight or ten years old, and particularly vintage ports, will require decanting because a deposit of solid matter will have precipitated out of them. It is very risky to open a bottle of this age if it has been recently carried around or subjected to any other form of agitation. Much better to let it rest in peace for a couple of weeks before opening it. (All bottles should be stored on their sides in a cool place, ideally in racks, so that the underside of the cork remains in contact with the wine, thus preventing the cork from drying out, and possibly imparting musty flavours to the wine.) The day before you intend to serve it, stand the bottle upright so that the sediment will fall to the bottom.

Ideally, the process of decanting should take place by candlelight – that is to say, with the wine being poured out in front of a candle flame. This is not in order to add a layer of Vincent Price-type atmosphere, but so that as the end of the bottle nears, the first traces of sediment to appear in the stream of wine may be clearly seen, prompting you to stop pouring. If only a little remains in the bottle, throw it away. If there is at least half a glass left, the rest may be strained through a fine material. Clean muslin is the best medium for this; the filter-papers from a coffee-maker are the worst option as they strip the wine of some of its body. Although nightmarishly messy, a couple of thicknesses of ordinary kitchen roll will work, but you need to ensure that it isn't at all perfumed, as that too will inevitably ruin the wine.

Keeping Leftovers

If you inhabit the kind of household where a bottle of wine is typically left unfinished at the end of a meal, consider moving. Otherwise, on occasions where too much of a good wine has been opened, and it deserves a better fate than going into tomorrow's gravy, keep it.

Dry white wines generally break down much more quickly than any other type. Put the cork back in the bottle and return it to the fridge, but be sure to drink it the following evening. Red wines will last somewhat longer, provided the cork is put back in. We have occasionally come across forgotten part-bottles that were recorked as many as five days before, and the wine within was still in perfectly drinkable condition. Indeed, in the case of many a raw young red, they may be positively improved by this treatment, but we wouldn't recommend making a systematic habit of it.

Unfinished sparklers need a champagne-saver. This is a small device like a large crown cap with a clip on the side. It creates an airtight seal when driven into the top of the bottle, but the wine must, even so, be finished within the next 24 hours. An old mystical belief, that suspending a silver spoon in the neck of a bottle preserves the fizz, may confidently be laid to rest. It doesn't work.

In the case of red wines only, unfinished bottles may be frozen. As long as there is at least a third gone, put the corks back in and stand them upright (if practical) in the freezer. They can be thawed out naturally and will taste no different. In an absolute emergency, they may be defrosted in the microwave oven, but it is vital to remove any lead foil or capsule from the bottle as metal and microwaves most decidedly do not mix. If in doubt, don't.

A variety of gadgets for saving leftover wine is available. The Vacu-Vin, which sucks the harmful air out of the bottle before sealing the wine, has its devotees, but natural cork will do the trick quite as efficiently. The synthetic corks increasingly seen nowadays are typically made of an unyielding plastic compound and will not go back into the neck of the bottle once drawn. A reusable cork stopper is the answer to this. Screwtops present no such problems, and are being heavily promoted as we write, as the wave of the future – and not just for the cheapest Vino Collapso, but for fine wines too.

Keeping Fortified Wines

It is not unreasonably assumed that fortified wines will keep for far longer than table wines once opened. Indeed, the nineteenth-century habit of getting through a further whole bottle of fortified wine at the end of a dinner has now largely passed into history, and so a bottle is quite likely to make many appearances in the course of its career in your drinks cabinet. In the great majority of cases, this is fine. The sweeter, darker and richer the style of wine, the tougher it is.

However (and this is a big however), pale, dry styles of sherry such as fino and manzanilla must be finished much more quickly. They should always be served well-chilled anyway, and so the part-bottles must be returned to the fridge, but they should not be made to pant on longer than about a week. After this period, they will start to taste stale, a calamity that has already befallen probably the greater part of all the dry sherry served in restaurants and bars in the UK at any given time. If you doubt your capacity to get through a whole bottle of pale dry sherry in a week, buy half-bottles. That is what they are for.

Madeira is probably the hardiest of all the fortified wines, and may be kept in the cupboard for years without coming to any significant harm. (We find it too irresistible to keep that long.) Vermouth, which is not only fortified but aromatised with an apothecary's shop of herbs and spices, will also sit in this neglected state without sulking, but the dry white styles should again be kept in the fridge.

Tasting Technique

As this book is about drinking wine with food, you don't need to concern yourself unduly with the professional tasting ritual for wine. However, at other times, it does immeasurably enhance the enjoyment of wines, and is worth having a go at when you can be perfectly sure nobody is going to catch you at it. We do it all the time, almost unconsciously, but then we're funny like that.

The first thing is appearance, which can tell you a lot about a wine. Tilting the glass away from you until it is almost horizontal will reveal the width and hue of the 'rim'. The wine's clarity, brightness, depth of colour and any bubbles of carbon dioxide are best seen by looking at it from above, with the glass standing on a table. As a general rule, wine should look bright and clear, although a certain very faint cloudiness is not necessarily a worrying sign. Many fine wines in the modern era are bottled unfiltered (which is to say that they haven't had the fine suspension of solid particles in them removed by one of various methods). Over-zealous filtration can strip some of the feeling of body or richness out of a wine, so avoiding the filtering process altogether enhances the amount of concentrated flavour.

Hold the glass against a white or light background to give a general impression of the colour. Then take your first sniff before you swirl the wine. Holding the glass by the stem or the foot, gently swish the wine around. Most right-handed people move the glass anticlockwise; left-handers find it easier clockwise. Either way, very little movement is required. Swirl the wine and hold it up to the light. Examine the 'tears' or 'legs' that run down the insides of the glass. Are they large or small? Slow or fast-moving? These attributes determine the viscosity, weight, alcohol and sugar in the wine. Heavy, viscous tears in the glass are a sign of a wine of great concentration (very sweet dessert wines have very thick tears as a result of their high sugar levels).

Swirl again and sniff the wine, using short sniffs and deeper ones, very gentle sniffs and much sharper ones. Concentrate on the aromas, and what they remind you of. Note down your thoughts if you wish.

Taste the wine by taking a reasonably generous mouthful. 'Chew' it around your mouth for a few seconds, and then purse your lips and suck some air into your mouth to aerate the wine. If you are keeping a note, write down your description of the wine's components: its level of acidity, fruit flavours, amount of oak influence (if applicable), and – in the case of red wines – the degree of tannin the wine possesses. A wine that has been matured in oak barrels will display a strong note of vanilla in the aroma and flavour, and in the case of white wines, will be on the darker, straw-gold side of the spectrum. Since new oak barrels represent a formidable outlay for a wine producer, the evident presence of oak in the wine gives a clear indication of the quality category it is being positioned in. On the other hand, it is possible to have too much of a good thing, and too many wines are spoiled by being kept for too long in oak, so that the effect is a kind of top-heaviness in the wine, with a weight of rich wood flavour bearing down on too slight a supporting structure in the wine itself. By the same token, the absence of oak is by no means an indicator of a less good wine. Some grape varieties, despite the efforts of a handful of mould-breaking experimentalists, just don't take to oak (these include wines made from Riesling, Gewürztraminer, Muscat and most Sauvignon Blanc).

Corked and Faulty Wine
The most common fault encountered in wine is cork taint, which is caused by a chemical used in treating the cork

having reacted with and spoiled the wine. This obviously only applies to those wines that are sealed with real cork, and not those with screwtops or those wretched plastic stoppers that have a habit of getting stuck fast in the top. Since corked wine is wine that's gone bad, you should no more accept it and pay for it than you would a box of mouldy strawberries. Whether you've bought it from a high-street retailer such as a supermarket, or a specialist wine merchant, stick the cork back in and take it back at the first opportunity. [Ask them to taste it themselves and confirm the problem, if they look at all doubtful.] In a restaurant, send it back if you are not happy with the first taste. Since cork taint generally only affects single bottles at random, you can fairly confidently try another bottle of the same thing. However, if that turns out to be off too, the chances are that the producer has unknowingly bought a bad batch of cork, in which case switch to something else.

One day, all wine will be bottled in screwtop bottles, which is generally held to be a good thing by many wine commentators. It obviously sidesteps the risk of cork taint, but isn't quite as aesthetically pleasing. If you are still rather attached to real cork, according to these commentators, you are evidently the sort of half-baked neanderthal who prefers hard-covered books to paperbacks and has a phone with a rotary dial. We couldn't possibly comment. While the case for screwtops has been vigorously put, the incidence of cork taint has been childishly exaggerated. At a conservative estimate, we would suggest that around 3-4% of cork-sealed bottles are affected.

Still, it's worth gaining confidence in being able to spot a corked wine. Its main odour is a damp-smelling mustiness, a little like unwashed dishcloths or perhaps the blue mould that forms on old bread, if you can remember back to student days. Once smelled, it is never forgotten, and even though some wines may be only very slightly tainted, you will come to recognise it even when quite faint. Occasionally, if a bottle is only just 'on the turn', so to speak, it may not be apparent to the nose, but will make its presence felt when the wine is tasted. When more advanced, it completely obliterates any of the fresh fruit scents that a wine should have.

Other, less frequent, wine faults are: *oxidation*, where air has got into the bottle via a faulty seal, or through its having been left open for too long (as in a bar where it is being sold by the glass over a number of days) or perhaps because the wine wasn't properly protected from exposure to air when being made, leaving it tasting flat and tired, sometimes oddly metallic, and disturbingly turning the colour of a white wine into something that looks more like Lucozade; *sulphide*, in which the sulphur dioxide used as an antioxidant in most wines has bonded with hydrogen to produce hydrogen sulphide, the telltale sign of which is a stinkbomb-like whiff of rotten egg; and *tartrate precipitation*, caused when a wine, whose natural tartaric acid wasn't fully stabilised before bottling, deposits a mass of blackish, sour-tasting crystals, which will usually only be encountered when the last glass is poured out.

In the case of oxidation, the wine is as irreversibly ruined as a corked wine is. Send it back. Sulphide, especially in a young wine, often wafts away with air contact after a few minutes, but if it persists, then send that back too. Tartrate precipitation is quite harmless and doesn't affect the flavour of the wine, even though it can make for a rather crunchy final mouthful if you don't spot it. When returning wine, though, remember that it isn't the fault of either the retailer or the restaurant, so don't wipe the floor with them. They bought the wine in good faith, and will now have the delicate task of informing the winemaker and getting a credit note. Or, more likely, they will take the view that it isn't worth the bother, and write it off as a loss.

2

GRAPES

No factor in winemaking influences the flavour and character of the finished wine more than the grape variety or varieties from which it is made. With the emergence of the non-European wine countries to commercial prominence in recent years, that fact has moved from being a piece of arcane specialist knowledge to become a matter of public familiarity. This has undoubtedly benefited the newer countries. Everybody knows what sort of style a wine labelled Chardonnay will have. Fewer know that a French white wine labelled Mercurey is also Chardonnay.

A handful – a couple of handfuls, perhaps – of the most important grapes used in making wine is worth becoming familiar with. Not only will you find yourself treading more surely in the tangled thickets of the modern wine industry, but your confidence in choosing the appropriate wine to go with a planned menu will be immeasurably enhanced. Eventually, certain dishes, certain sauces, even certain seasonings, just seem to shout out for a particular wine, and more often than not, it will be a particular grape variety or blend that you hit on, as opposed to a specific geographical area. What that lamb wants is 'a good oaky Tempranillo,' you will think. As opposed to 'a three-year-old Reserva red from Navarra'.

In this chapter, we offer an alphabetical guide to the grapes you need to know. These are not necessarily always the most widely grown internationally, although those that answer that description are all included. The wine industries of southern Europe – especially Spain and Italy – have a number of varieties that are of central importance to their wine industries, and only appear peripherally and experimentally, if at all, in other regions. Nonetheless, because they make some of the finest, gastronomically indispensable wines in Spain and Italy themselves, they deserve a place at the top table.

A wine made from a single grape variety is known in the trade as a varietal wine, but don't let this grape-led approach allow you to forget that a lot of the world's classic wines are blends of two or more grapes. The wines of Bordeaux, the Rhône, Champagne, Rioja, Chianti and most of Portugal are blends of different varieties, and it won't take an unduly pedantic reader to see that the business of food-and-wine matching would be considerably the poorer without those.

Against the listing for each variety, we have given an indication of where it is grown, and the scents and flavours typically to be expected from it, followed by some of the kinds of cooking or specific dishes that best suit it. In effect, you are being introduced to the main business of this book in reverse. It regularly happens that we seize on a bottle that looks too good to miss, and then devise a menu around it, as opposed to letting the wines follow the food. This approach is equally good fun, and if you decide to try it, this chapter should send you boldly off in the direction of your cookery books.

WHITE VARIETIES
Aligoté A minor white grape of Burgundy, its wine varietally labelled as Bourgogne Aligoté (or Bourgogne Aligoté de Bouzeron, a particularly good enclave within its catchment

area). Light lemony nose, often with a suggestion of sour cream about it. Assertive acidity, best caught young. Drinks well with cold-water shellfish, either as *plateau de fruits de mer*, or in salads. Mayonnaise won't faze it; vinaigrette more of a challenge (make it with lemon juice, rather than vinegar).

Arneis A speciality of the Piedmont region of northwest Italy. Ordinary ones may well taste as neutral as the generality of Italian dry white. From better growers, it has a distinct aroma of tart pears, and produces a wine with a pleasing silky texture. Drink with antipasti dishes involving cured meats, creamy-sauced pasta dishes, or grilled white fish.

Chardonnay King of the white wine grape varieties, master of all it surveys in wine regions ranging from northern California to the South Island of New Zealand, and from one side of Europe to the other, not forgetting its original heartland, Burgundy, where it makes some of the world's most unforgettable dry white wines. In itself, a rather neutral-tasting variety, its affinity with oak is what has made it the brightest star in the firmament.

Unoaked, expect a delicate, lemony, perhaps appley white with softish acidity and not much finish. (The classic exception is Chablis, where a cool northern climate bestows on it sharper acidity, richer, creamier flavours and the capacity to age.) When given a modest period of contact with oak, it begins to take on a range of more exotic flavours – peach, vanilla, soft spices such as cinnamon or nutmeg. Oak-aged for the better part of a year, it can become hugely rich, full of melted butter, honey, clotted cream, and often displaying a savoury, smoky edge derived from the charred inner surfaces of the barrels it matures in.

Chardonnay is a hugely versatile wine for matching with food, which is why it tends to crop up so often on the world's dinner tables and why restaurant wine lists are so chock-full of it. The unoaked styles are best with simple shellfish or freshwater fish dishes, summer salads, and bowls of pasta dressed with little more than a dribble of pesto or garlic butter. Lightly oaked, it will take richer sauces made with cream or crème fraîche, and the denser-textured species of fish, such as salmon, turbot, sea bass and monkfish. The heavily oaked versions are best with white meats such as good corn-fed chicken, turkey and guinea-fowl, happily standing up to roasts as the occasion demands. A piece of pork tenderloin sautéed and served with a strong mustard sauce is fine too, but roast pork tends to be better off with a red wine.

Chenin Blanc A native grape of the western and central Loire Valley, also very popular in South Africa, where it used to be known more widely as Steen. Chenin is one of those rather special white grapes that makes wines across the entire stylistic spectrum, from razor-sharp, high-acid, dry wines, through demi-sec (medium-dry) in-betweenies, all the way up to syrupy dessert wines, with a brief digression into bone-dry fizz along the way. The sweetest wines have all the luscious, honey-dripping richness one might expect from such creations, with lashings of oozy-ripe peach and apricot fruit flavours too. At its driest, though – especially in such Loire wines as the sec versions of Vouvray and Montlouis – its scents and flavours can be a little challenging. The textbook tasting note, wet wool, is a good one; it is often that precise aroma that comes off the woolly jumper you peel off just after coming in from a cloudburst, and drape over the bathroom radiator to dry. There is a dry nuttiness to it as well, like freshly shelled walnuts, and occasionally something a bit more upsetting, the distinctly sicky smell of powdered Parmesan that's been sitting in the cupboard for too long.

Its slicing acidity makes dry Chenin a good match for anything with a lot of fat to cut through. It's not bad with avocado, and makes a clean breast of salt cod brandade, where the rough, mousse-like texture of the dish needs a sharp wine. As demi-sec, it can be good with savoury dishes that have a touch of obvious sweetness to them, such as honey-glazed baked ham, or lighter-textured game birds with a fruit note in the sauce or dressing. The very sweet wines are best with desserts like glazed fruit tarts, egg-based dishes such as crème brûlée, or the stronger varieties of blue cheese, like Roquefort, Ireland's Cashel Blue or Beenleigh Blue from Devon. Drink sparkling Vouvray as a palate-cleansing aperitif.

Colombard A fairly undistinguished white variety, widely used in the Vin de Pays des Côtes de Gascogne of south-west France, and blended with the more illustrious likes of Chardonnay in South Africa, Australia and California. Simple, lemony flavours in the cooler climates, taking on a slightly richer note of sweetcorn in the hotter ones.

Gewürztraminer (aka Traminer in northeast Italy, Austria and parts of Germany) A most peculiar, pink-skinned grape that may have originated in central Europe, but now has its first home in Alsace. Also grown over the border in Germany, in southern and eastern Europe (where it's also often known simply as Traminer), and enterprisingly in many of the southern hemisphere countries. Makes the gamut of styles from dry to sweet, although its dry versions are never the driest of the dry, especially not in Alsace. The German prefix *Gewürz* means 'spicy', and the wines characteristically do their best to live up to that billing, evoking anything from ginger and cinnamon to cloves, cardamom and nutmeg. Add to that a bracing fruit like pink grapefruit or nectarine (banana in the sweeter versions), and a divertingly cosmetic perfume like scented soap or expensive talcum powder, and it will be seen that this is the most singular, and singularly recognisable, grape variety of the lot.

The driest versions are particularly good with highly spiced east Asian cooking, notably Chinese and Thai, where their velvety texture and assertive flavours take both chilli-hot and sweet-and-sour seasonings in their stride. It's less good with Indian cooking, but by no means disastrous. Otherwise, Gewürztraminer makes a fine accompaniment to the richly flavoured pâtés and terrines of its pre-eminent region, Alsace. It comes into its own with a thick slice of *terrine de foie gras*, but is almost as good with any robustly textured liver pâté. Drink the sweet wines (labelled Vendange Tardive or, sweeter still, Sélection de Grains Nobles) in the same contexts as you would a sweet Chenin (see above).

Grüner Veltliner An indigenous white grape of Austria that has acquired something of a claim to fame. Gives wines with high alcohol in a stony-dry style, but with an appealing citrus tang like oranges, backed up by a twist of peppery spice. Good with the often fatty, pork-based cooking of its native country, where its cutting acidity comes in handy, or perhaps with roast poultry. Its relative weightiness seems to make it a better bet with white meats, anyway, than with fish.

Marsanne Important white grape of the northern Rhône Valley, where it nearly always appears blended with its sister variety, Roussanne. Also increasingly visible as a trendy varietal from Australia. Delicately spicy in a cinnamony sort of way in the Rhône. Fat and blowsy from

Australia, with big tropical fruit flavours – mango, papaya, banana. Suits the spicy complexity of Pacific Rim cooking well, the kind of wine to reach for when odd combinations of ingredients (shellfish and fruit, meat and chocolate) seem to defeat other wines.

Müller-Thurgau Workhorse grape of the German wine heartlands, crossed from Riesling and Sylvaner (see entries). Once very widely grown, now rapidly dwindling, in New Zealand. Can make fairly workaday dry wines, or sweeter ones with a sight more personality. Doesn't have much fruit, but often has a light floral whiff that can be pleasing enough for a minute or two. Not one for your best dishes, but does reasonably well with a salad of baby artichokes in a mustardy, garlicky dressing.

Muscadet The eponymous grape variety of the Muscadet district at the western end of the Loire was also historically known as Melon de Bourgogne, on account of its shape and its region of origin. Water-white wines of crunching acidity, and little or no fruit beyond a slight suggestion of tart green apple-peel. Some, labelled *sur lie* (meaning 'on the lees'), are held on their fermentation sediment for a period before bottling, which imparts a very faintly softer quality ('creamier' is overdoing it) to the texture. Best served ice-cold with platters of Atlantic shellfish and lashings of mayonnaise.

Muscat A family of grapes, rather than a single variety, the undisputed head of which is Muscat Blanc à Petits Grains. Grown in Alsace, Germany and southern Europe, but now more or less throughout the world too. Classically produces sweet, sticky wines that are often fortified with a slug of grape spirit (e.g. Muscat de Beaumes-de-Venise), but also makes more delicate sweet versions, labelled 'Late-Picked' in the English-speaking countries. Alsace makes some fine dry versions of Muscat. Other dry Muscats can be horrid, with an aspiriny, chemical aftertaste, but the Alsace ones are full of that regional spice character. The sweeter it gets, the more recognisably like the fresh Muscat grape it tastes, that juicy, sweet grapiness often underlined with a festive splash of orange. Australia also makes a unique style of fortified wine from it, Liqueur Muscat, a dark brown, marmaladey potion of enormous concentration and power.

Drink dry Alsace Muscat with the same foods as dry Gewürztraminer (it's quite as good with foie gras). The late-picked, slightly sweet ones are good with lightly dressed fresh fruit salads, or featherlight lemon tart, while the very sweet Sélection wines should be served with richer, stickier desserts. Save the Australian Liqueur Muscats for anything densely chocolatey (a chocolate-and-orange dessert even better), or sip them as digestifs once all the eating has been done.

Pinot Blanc Fairly neutral-tasting grape of eastern France: varietal in Alsace, a bit-part player in Burgundy, known as Weissburgunder in Germany. Has made inroads into Italy, and crops up here and there outside Europe. Its patchy take-up is largely accounted for by its lack of character. Even in Alsace, it is merely gently appley, perhaps slightly milky, low in acidity and quickly forgotten. Will serve as any all-purpose dry white (it would make a much better house white than the white that most neighbourhood restaurants stock), but best with simple dishes such as relatively plain pasta or risotto.

Pinot Gris/Grigio Another Alsace varietal that plays a supporting role in Germany (as Ruländer), but has made more of a name for itself in Italy. Indeed, as far as brand recognition is concerned, Italy has now become its *locus* *classicus*. Fashionable in the northwest corner of the USA too (Oregon and Washington State). Good Alsace versions, often labelled Tokay-Pinot Gris, bring out all the fat, spicy character of it, matching the regional spice tones with a butteriness almost like Chardonnay and a citric tang like clementines. Much Italian Grigio tastes of nothing, perhaps a dollop of cooked apple if you're lucky, but a few producers have coaxed some aromatic personality out of it, generally by making it from low-yielding vines. Like Gewürztraminer, Muscat and Riesling, it will rot in the right conditions to produce sensational dessert wines.

Drink the better dry wines with those pâtés and terrines again, but also, the meatier types of white fish such as cod and monkfish (especially if there is some bacon involved in the preparation) and richly sauced poultry. Corn-fed chicken sautéed with mushrooms and onions in a creamy white wine sauce is a memorable match with Pinot Gris. The dessert wines will take the same treatments as the other Sélection-style wines (see Muscat).

Riesling The VIP grape of German and Alsace wines has been exported all around the world now. In Germany, its best manifestations are all sweet wines, from the delicate late-picked style to the fully rounded, intensely sweet dessert version. Alsace, and many of the non-European countries, also makes a bone-dry version with plenty of snappy acidity. It's that acidity that helps it to age, and which also gives the very sweet wine exemplary balance. Riesling very often has a pronounced scent of lime, particularly in the dry and off-dry wines, while the sweetest ones display the juicy muskiness of ultra-ripe peaches and apricots, allied to the tangy stickiness of lime or lemon marmalade.

While the very sweetest wines work best with desserts, as for Muscat and Gewürztraminer, the drier versions are extremely versatile wines. They are good with shellfish dishes such as ceviche, or in any fruity or exotically flavoured dressings. The complex, forthright spicing of Indian cooking holds no terror for Riesling, and the lime-scented seasonings in Thai food might have been invented for it. Its acidity makes it a very efficient foil to oily fish such as smoked mackerel or herring. In short, its wines are probably the most versatile white wines available – more so even than Chardonnay.

Sauvignon Blanc An international grape with its roots in the upper Loire Valley, Sauvignon has become especially trendy in New Zealand, but it also shows well in central Europe, South Africa, parts of Chile and Australia and, to a lesser extent, in California. At its best, it is an exhilaratingly fruity wine, with tart green fruits such as apples and gooseberries in abundance, backed up by more exotic notes (mango, passion-fruit, even blackcurrant) in the southern hemisphere. Strong acidity makes it a good match for oily dressings, so it is one of the summer salad wines *par excellence*. It also makes an unimpeachable match with asparagus – served simply steamed with melted butter or with hollandaise – and with goats' cheese, either fresh or toasted and served on salad leaves. The ripeness of its fruit makes it a good partner for bitter leaves such as rocket, radicchio and endive.

Semillon Originally from Bordeaux, where it is blended with Sauvignon to make dry and sweet whites, but has also carved out a niche for itself as a dry varietal in Australia, most notably the Hunter Valley. When dry, it produces an acerbic, nutty white with a slight citrus tang, and a deceptive suggestion of toastiness, often seeming to have been oaked when it hasn't. Noble-rotted Semillons, made, like those Alsace Sélections, from grapes that have been allowed to shrivel on the vine, can be masterpieces of honeyed richness, teeming with ripe orchard fruits and the vanilla creaminess of cask-ageing. The Sauternes and Barsac districts of Bordeaux are the most internationally celebrated names for this style of Semillon. These are best with soft-textured, luxurious desserts such as crème brûlée, mousses, bavarois and crème caramel. The dry wines are usually sturdy enough to stand up to white meats, even the lighter-fleshed game birds, or at least the meatier types of fish. A wild mushroom risotto with Parmesan and maybe truffle oil is a good restaurant dish to go with dry Australian Semillon.

Sylvaner Minor grape of Alsace and Germany, of no great charm. Its wines tend to have a pungently vegetal quality, quite like steamed cabbage, a little of which goes a long way. The pre-eminent German example, Frankenwein, is probably most at home with pork and sauerkraut.

Trebbiano Very widely used in Italy's dry white wines, either on its own or as the greater part of a blend. Produces wines of no noticeable distinction, tasting light and crisp, but not at all of fruit. That said, there are gastronomic contexts in which these wines (e.g. Soave, Frascati, Orvieto, etc.) are appropriate, such as with oily dressings or where the strength of flavour or seasoning in a dish would easily denude a more complex wine of its subtleties, and only a common-or-garden, fresh dry white is what's needed. Their relative lightness makes them good lunchtime wines.

Verdejo Speciality grape of the northern Spanish region of Rueda. Produces light whites with acid grip and a leafy, herbaceous flavour. Works well in the same sorts of contexts as Sauvignon Blanc (see above).

Verdicchio Indigenous to eastern central Italy (as in Verdicchio dei Castelli di Jesi). Crisp but fairly neutral wines, perhaps popular for the same reasons that Pinot Grigio is. For salads, white fish and goats' cheeses.

Vernaccia A central and southern Italian variety whose most famous wine is Tuscany's Vernaccia di San Gimignano. Lightly creamy, lemony style, sometimes with a finishing touch of almond. Best with baked white fish, or the lightest poultry dishes (poached, rather than fried or roasted, chicken).

Viognier Almost limitlessly fashionable in recent years, Viognier started life in an enclave of the northern Rhône, where it makes the expensive but gorgeous Condrieu. Now appearing all over the known vinous world as an alternative to Chardonnay, it makes wines with pure apricot fruit, bright lemony acidity, heroic alcohol levels and more than a hint of scented spice – touches of Indian spice are not uncommon. In the hotter countries, it takes on a less than alluring honey-and-lemon combination, which may make it taste more like something for a sore throat. Like its northern Rhône counterpart, Marsanne, it is a dream wine with Pacific Rim or 'fusion' food, where there are often cascades of sour, spicy, fruity, edgy flavours all going on in the same dish.

RED VARIETIES
Barbera Attractive red grape of northwest Italy, where it appears on labels with its district of origin (e.g. Barbera d'Asti). Also showing well in California and Argentina. The wines are richly coloured, and have a sharp-edged fruit flavour like cherries. Like all acidic wines, Barbera works well with dishes where fat is an issue. Roast duck is a good partner for it, but it also suits pork recipes with some fruit content.

Cabernet Franc One of the extras in Bordeaux, but came into its own a long time ago as a varietal red in the central Loire Valley. Some varietal wines are made in northern Italy and the Americas too. Those Loire reds, such as Chinon and Bourgueil, can be delicious, full of black-currant and raspberry fruit, held in check by light, but sharp tannins. It needs the warm, ripe years though. South of the Equator, it produces a much darker, richer wine, often indistinguishable from its cousin, Cabernet Sauvignon (see below). Italian versions are grassy-green in flavour, and featherlight.

Drink the Loire wines with French charcuterie. They are good with the pungent, offaly sausages known as *andouillettes*. Otherwise, roasted lighter meats are called for. The Chilean and Californian examples will happily take the darker red meats: beef, lamb, duck and so forth.

Cabernet Sauvignon The principal grape of red Bordeaux (known as claret), and the most important international red grape of them all. Classically, it is a fairly weighty, blackcurrant-scented red with heavy tannins when young, softening to deep and complex maturity as it ages. Even those countries where it once produced a lighter, more herbaceous style of red, such as Italy and New Zealand, are now getting to grips with it through better winemaking, and turning out richer, more healthily coloured wines. In Bordeaux, it has the telltale woody perfumes of cigar-boxes and pencil shavings, and there is sometimes a suggestion of garden mint, or more savoury herbs such as thyme. From Australia and California, its upfront purple fruit is generally supported by layers of creamy oak, adding a pronounced vanilla tinge to the finish.

Fine claret should be drunk, after it has been allowed a few years in the bottle to come to full maturity, with plainly served red meats. Roast lamb is best suited to it, but it will also come to no harm with beef or venison, as long as there is no sweet or spicy sauce to contend with. Other than that, almost any dark meat dishes will do: casseroles, braises, simply grilled steaks, even burgers made with 100% ground beef.

Cinsault/Mourvèdre/Carignan These are the supporting grapes in blends based on Syrah and Grenache (qv), cropping up all over the southern Rhône, the Languedoc and Roussillon. They all have varying degrees of peppery or gingery spice, and contribute to the robustly full-bodied feel of these southern wines.

Dolcetto Another of Piedmont's grapes, Dolcetto makes light and fruity, though deeply coloured, wines of instant appeal for drinking young – a sort of Beaujolais Nouveau without the tears caused by indigestible acids. Expect unabashed blueberry fruit, and sharp but balanced acidity. These wines go well with light meats in fruity dressings or sauces, and also with soft cow's-milk cheeses, such as Camembert, Brie or their Italian counterparts.

Gamay The red grape of Beaujolais, occasionally tried outside its homeland, but never destined to produce great wine, so it hasn't become a must-grow like many other French originals. Tart, featherlight reds with sharp cherry or strawberry fruit, often tasting a little confected like boiled sweets. The richer wines made by certain Beaujolais villages (Moulin-à-Vent and Morgon) age to a gently gamey maturity. Drink with soft cheeses, seared salmon or roasted white meats.

Grenache/Garnacha Grown worldwide, but its twin stamping-grounds are southern France (the southern Rhône, the Languedoc and Roussillon) and northern

Spain (principally Rioja, Navarra and Penedés). The Spanish call it Garnacha; in France, and everywhere else, it is known as Grenache. Nearly always blended with one or two of the other traditional grapes of these regions, such as Mourvèdre, Cinsault, Carignan and Syrah, the wines are typically midweight with a slight spicy edge like black pepper or even ginger, light cherry fruit and moderate tannins. Denser, richer versions are made throughout these regions too, though, as exemplified by certain wines from Châteauneuf-du-Pape, Gigondas and the Sangre de Toro blends of Torres. Also handy for light, strawberry-perfumed rosés.

The richer wines are good with highly spiced red meat dishes: the likes of peppered steak and even Indian lamb dishes are good bets. Save the rosés for pink fish or meat such as salmon or ham.

Malbec A strolling player in Bordeaux, but pre-eminent in Cahors in France's Lot Valley, and something of a signature wine in Argentina's Mendoza region. Midweight tannins, ripe damson fruit and sometimes a hint of something spicy like liquorice are its calling cards. It works supremely well with both beef, which the Argentinians consume in heroic quantities, and with duck, especially the duck confit traditional in southwest France, and its most famous dish, *cassoulet*.

Merlot Cabernet Sauvignon's partner in Bordeaux, but hugely important as a varietal in its own right all over the world. Often thought to be the soft-toned good cop to Cabernet's rock-hard tough guy, but is quite capable of flexing its muscles unassisted in the hotter countries. Typically has soft purple fruit aromas, plums and black-berries, backed up by chocolatey richness and a whiff of smoke if oak-aged. Cooler climates leave it tasting a bit feeble – best avoided. Good with softer-textured meat dishes, such as poultry and roast pork, and with hard cow's-milk cheeses of the Cheddar type, but the heavier Californian versions will rub along well with more sinewy red meats.

Nebbiolo Piedmont's finest red grape is used in two of Italy's monumental classic wines, Barolo and Barbaresco. Plantings elsewhere are still at a purely speculative stage. Thundering with tannin in its youth (and well into its middle-age too), it has a sublimely complex array of scents from freshly mixed tar through Turkish Delight to dark, bitter chocolate. Headily scented, well-hung game is what it's crying out for, and it goes well with any red meats that have been flavoured with truffles. Those crushing tannins will seem extra-tough if you try to pair it with a particularly chewy cut of meat, though.

Pinot Noir The red grape of Burgundy, but grown throughout the world now, with vastly varying degrees of success. At its best, it produces a light-textured, raspberry-ish or cherryish wine that gathers to itself a strongly gamey hint – like well-hung meat – as it ages. Even if it doesn't go gamey, there's usually an underlying savoury note like beef stock in it. In cooler climates, it can seem lean, green and pointless, but California and New Zealand are now turning out some excellent Pinots.
A mature burgundy from one of the richer appellations (e.g. Gevrey-Chambertin, Morey St-Denis or Pommard) is the best possible match with roast game birds such as grouse, partridge, wood-pigeon or pheasant. It's also good with duck in fruity sauces, where its acidity helps to cut any fat, with poached or baked salmon, and with those soft, creamy white cheeses (pre-eminently with a ripe Epoisses from the Burgundy region).

Pinotage A red speciality of South Africa crossed from
Pinot Noir and Cinsault. Tends to produce a light-to-
midweight red with cranberry or redcurrant fruit, but
more often than not with a disturbing, hard, burnt-tasting
edge that limits its appeal with food.

Sangiovese Of predominant importance in northern and
central Italy, principally Tuscany where it is the main grape
of Chianti and (under its pseudonym Brunello) of
Brunello di Montalcino. Much Chianti is light and cur-
ranty in style, perhaps with a fugitive waft of sun-dried
tomato, and with a peppery edge on the palate. The colour
fades out of it quite early, leaving it looking faintly orange.
Brunello has more staying power, but also commands a
loftier price. Drink Sangiovese-based blends with tomato-
sauced pasta dishes, anything with lots of herbs, with cold
meats such as carpaccio (garnished perhaps with shaved
Parmesan), and with meaty risottos. It is virtually the only
thing that works really well with high-street pizza.

Syrah/Shiraz Like Grenache/Garnacha, this grape strad-
dles the Franco-Spanish border, appearing in much the
same blends, and in France also as a solo performer in the
reds of the northern Rhône (e.g. Hermitage and Côte-
Rôtie). It has also become a superstar of the Australian
wine scene, where it makes big, strapping varietals, as well
as some bizarre but likeable red fizz. Much grown
throughout the Americas and South Africa. Makes good,
fruity rosé as well. Syrah is its French name, also used in
California, while Shiraz is its synonym in Australia and
South Africa. Chile uses either name, depending on the
producer.
In the northern Rhône, the wines are full of the scent of
freshly milled black pepper, decked out with a bouquet of
violets and roses to boot. The fruit is dark, like black

plums and damsons, and the tannin can be pretty fierce. In Australia, the spice notes tend to disappear in favour of creamy oak, and (as is typical in the Barossa Valley) a beguiling topnote of spearmint.

Venison, beef, duck and the other dark red meats are what a good Syrah requires, and it takes to spicy seasonings like a duck to pepper. Australian and Californian wines are perfect with barbecued meats (steaks, sausages and the like) and, in the case of the former, make a gastronomically precise match with kangaroo meat.

Tempranillo Grown throughout Spain under multifarious pseudonyms, but of particular significance in blended wines in the northern regions of Rioja, Navarra and Ribera del Duero. Its wines range from midweight to densely rich, passing along the fruit continuum from red (strawberries and cherries) to purple (blackberries and blackcurrants). Usually treated to extended oak ageing, it often has plenty of creamy vanilla all over it, balanced by well-defined acidity.

In Spain, nothing but a Tempranillo-based blend will do with the unashamedly fatty roast lamb of the northern regions. It's also good, though, with hard cheeses such as the sheep's-milk Manchego, and piquant salads of cured meats.

Zinfandel Speciality grape of California, where it makes a range of styles, though mostly at the rich and heavy end of the spectrum. Scents and flavours of blueberries and raspberries, allied to a strange sweet spice character, and a distinct note of tea leaves. Drink classically with barbecued meats, and with strongly seasoned grilled meats such as prime beef fillet and lamb cutlets.

3

APERITIFS

The purpose of an aperitif is to prime the appetite for the food to come. In its French derivation, it literally means an 'opener', in the sense of opening up the digestive system for what it is about to receive. It is also, of course, coincidentally the opener to a gastronomic occasion, and as such deserves to be chosen with care.

We are of the unshakeable opinion that wines and wine-based drinks make the best aperitifs. A watered whisky or dark rum with a splash of soda in it are perfectly commodious drinks that we can be persuaded to take in certain circumstances, but in terms of sheer efficiency at doing the job, wines are the thing. Some drink a pint of beer before dinner, which – unless you are very used to it – runs the risk of bloating the stomach at precisely the wrong moment. Others down three G&Ts, which has the air more of a drinking session curtailed than the curtain-raiser to sitting down to dinner.

The two greatest appetite-whetters in the world are pale dry sherry and champagne. Note that both of these drinks are dry. Sourness and bitterness are fine in a pre-dinner drink, but sweetness is the one flavour type to be shunned. This is because a sweet taste has a satiating effect on the palate, informing it briskly that it needn't bother preparing

itself to eat now. It is why we eat desserts at the end of a
meal rather than at the beginning, and is also why a sweet
snack such as a chocolate bar helps to assuage mid-
morning or mid-afternoon hunger pangs. In France,
famously, they drink cheap grades of port, or else their
own dessert wines such as Sauternes or Muscat de
Beaumes-de-Venise, before a meal, and have done for
generations. There are many glories of French gastronomic culture, the assimilation of which has made the
cuisines of other countries richer than they would otherwise be, but this is not one of them. The best we can say is
that this unfathomable habit appears to be dying out with
the younger generation, who have increasingly turned to
other aperitifs instead, such as . . . er, beer. Still, putting
that unpleasantness behind us, we can turn triumphantly
to the sherry bottle.

SHERRY

All wine labelled 'sherry' has to come from the sherry
region of southern Spain. Pale dry sherries come in two
basic types: most is simply labelled Fino, and is made
around the towns of Jérez de la Frontera and Puerta de
Santa Maria, but there is also a geographically distinct
product made further up the Andalusian coast at Sanlúcar
de Barrameda, called Manzanilla. It is the same basic style
as Fino, anaemically pale-looking and desert-dry, but it is
generally held to have an even more savoury tang to it,
even a faintly salty smack derived, it is said, from the sea
air that wafts around the barrels. In practice, most people
would be hard put to spot the difference between the two
styles. Both, at their best, are utterly delicious. They are
not by and large expensive, but they should be treated with
kid gloves. Buy from a store with a high turnover to ensure
optimum freshness, chill the bottle well and drink it up
within a few days – a week at most – of opening.

The dryness of dry sherry is so supremely efficacious at honing the appetite that it is almost a cruelty to your guests not to serve something to nibble on with it. Salted nuts, such as cashews, pecans or almonds, are all fine, as are freshly bought marinated black or green olives. Avoid stuffed olives out of a bottle, as they tend to have a rather processed flavour. Otherwise, think tapas: strips of dry-cured Serrano ham, cubes of briny sheep's-milk feta cheese, little salty fish such as anchovies or smoked fish like salmon are all extremely appetising with pale dry sherry, but don't serve so much that the nibbles assume the dimensions of a starter, for fear of upsetting the overall balance of your menu plan.

There are bone-dry versions of the darker styles of sherry too. Amontillado, Palo Cortado and Oloroso tend to be thought of as ascending through the sweetness scale from mildly raisiny through toffeeish to unabashed treacle. It ain't necessarily so. Look for 'Seco' or 'Muy Seco' on the label, and give these darker dry styles a try. They will cost more, but offer a unique and unforgettable range of flavours, especially when served with nuts.

The other fortified wine that can work as an aperitif is the driest style of madeira, Sercial. Beware though: even though this is the driest madeira, it still has a fugitive twist of sweetness in it, balanced however with a note of freshening acidity.

Serve fortified wines in generous quantities. If you have a set of sherry schooners, take them to the charity shop forthwith. Banish all liqueur glasses, and serve sherry in ordinary wine glasses, in quantities of *very* slightly less than a normal glass of table wine. It is stronger than table wine, to be sure, but only just.

CHAMPAGNE AND SPARKLING WINES
To drink a glass of champagne before eating has become enormously chic in recent years, especially now that so

many restaurants have taken to offering sparklers by the glass. If we were being completely honest, it is ever so slightly less efficient as an appetite-whetter than sherry, because the palate needs a moment to adjust to the bubbles and the high acidity, but once it does, it will find itself sharpened by the dryness of a Brut champagne. Besides, no wine on earth is more guaranteed to lift the spirits and get everybody into the mood for a cordial evening than a glass of champagne. It creates a sense of occasion and allows your guests to luxuriate in the feeling of drinking something rather opulent at somebody else's expense, and there are few feelings more likely than that to add to the sum of human happiness.

Almost any style of champagne or sparkling wine will do, apart from the sweeter versions labelled as Demi-Sec and Rich. When drinking it as an aperitif, though, you may find that the lighter it is, the better, which tends to mean any wine with a high preponderance of Chardonnay in the blend, or indeed one exclusively made from that obliging grape. In Champagne, the latter are labelled Blanc de Blancs, and provided they haven't had too much bottle-age, these will be among the most delicately lemony sparkling wines of all. (With age, they take on a beguiling toasty creaminess, which is one of the greatest of all champagne experiences, but works a little better served with food than on its own.)

A pale pink rosé champagne is an appealing prospect, particularly on a hot summer's evening, but steer clear of the very dark pink specimens, which may have had a bit too much red wine added to them, and will taste correspondingly too leaden to make an attractive aperitif.

Other countries making a good fist of champagne-style sparkling wines these days include the USA (principally California), New Zealand, South Africa, Australia and England. Not all of these will necessarily be made by the same method as champagne – although many will – but the quality is often virtually as good. Serve these wines for their own particular styles, rather than looking to them to replicate the flavour of true champagne as closely as possible. All should be vigorously chilled. An ice bucket raises the tone of the occasion by several notches, and guards against the remainder of the bottle coming up to room temperature if your guests are notably slow drinkers.

Allow plenty of time for the aperitif period if you are serving an expensive sparkler. Too often, we have found ourselves ushered to the table with virtually a full glass still in hand – not in itself a cause for complaint, you might think, but a little distressing if the first course now being served is something full of sharp or spicy seasonings, which will then effectively kill off the subtleties of the wine. Even smoked salmon, often seen as one of its traditional partners, can overwhelm a delicately textured sparkler.

AROMATISED FORTIFIED WINES
Despite the fact that many wine commentators tend either to deride or at best ignore vermouth, we are not of that

stamp. Well-made dry vermouth from one of the better
French or Italian producers has its place as an aperitif,
perhaps not every time, or even very often, but certainly
once in a while. It should be served as cold as pale dry
sherry, perhaps with a cube or two of ice and a half-slice
or twist of lemon. Noilly Prat from the south of France is
a particularly fine product, containing a bewitching array
of fruit and herb flavourings that make it a genuinely
complex proposition. Avoid like the plague any cheap
supermarket own-label dry vermouth. Its cheapness
denotes that it has been bottled sub-strength (good vermouth should be about 17%) to qualify for a lower duty
rate, but also reliably indicates the amount of care that has
been taken in its manufacture. Cheaper sweet red ver-
mouths can be just about palatable, especially if mixed,
but remember we don't want a sweet aperitif. And the dry
white version will smell of school changing-rooms at the
end of gym, and will taste a sight worse.

As well as vermouth, there are various proprietary
fortified wine brands that make fine aperitifs. The best
among these is undoubtedly Suze, which is a bright yellow,
intensely bitter, wine-based aperitif flavoured with gentian
root. Think of the bitter taste of quinine in tonic water,
and then think bitterer. It does contain sugar to offset
some of the effect, but its bitter attack on the back of the
tongue is so pronounced that one hardly notices the
sweetening. Mix it with a little water and ice. If you can get
it, that is. Not much gets exported from its home country
of France, and none at all to the UK. If you are planning
a cross-Channel trip, though, try a bottle. It's well worth
the experiment.

Italy's bright red, bitter *aperitivo* Campari is a fine
product too. It is best served on ice with a splash of soda,
or perhaps a dash of freshly squeezed orange juice (prepared by your own fair hand, not poured from a carton),

with a half-slice or twist of orange.

Serve vermouth and Suze in small tumblers, or in what is known in cocktail circles as an Old-Fashioned glass, the squat, wide-mouthed glass in which the bourbon-based cocktail of the same name is generally served. Vermouth should be served in more or less the same quantities as sherry. Suze can afford to be a shorter nip, in acknowledgement of its wondrously concentrated bitterness.

COCKTAILS AND MIXED DRINKS

Certain of the traditional wine-based cocktails are worth serving from time to time, especially if you are a regular entertainer, as a way of ringing the changes. By these, we most emphatically do not mean the white wine spritzer, which is a drink for people who don't really like drinking. There is nothing wrong with not liking alcohol (as long as they persevere in trying as many different types as possible, in recognition of the fact that there will be something out there somewhere that they'll take a shine to), but it seems an odd recourse to get round the fact by asking for half a glass of white wine to be drowned in soda and diluted with ice in acknowledgement of their proclivities. If it's good wine, they must be made to understand that they are depriving others of their share.

A Kir is probably the best-known wine cocktail of them all, and consists in adding about a teaspoon of crème de cassis (blackcurrant liqueur) to a glass of well-chilled dry white wine. Classically, the wine should be Bourgogne Aligoté, but any high-acid, unoaked dry white will do. The drink should not be iced. Substitute champagne – or, probably better, a good sparkling wine – for the still white, and the drink becomes a Kir Royale. Alternatively, the recipe can be varied by trying other red or purple fruit-flavoured liqueurs, such as crème de mûre (blackberries), crème de myrtille (bilberries) or crème de framboise (raspberries).

The original Sherry Cocktail consists of a large measure of pale dry sherry, stirred in a mixing-jug with a couple of dashes of orange bitters and ice until the drink is cold enough to have misted the surface of the jug, and then strained into a cocktail glass. To give it an extra kick, you can add a couple of dashes of dry vermouth to the jug as well.

For an incomparably well-balanced and appetising aperitif, the Negroni cocktail is a winner. Stir equal measures of gin, Campari and sweet red vermouth in a jug with ice until very cold, and then pour with the ice into a whisky tumbler or 'rocks' glass. Add a squirt of soda water if you think it needs it (it doesn't), and garnish with a half-slice of orange.

WHITE WINE

The simplest aperitif of all is a glass of chilled white wine, perhaps a preview serving of the wine you are intending to have with the first course. It is best not to serve anything too heavy in texture or too oaky as an opener, but a light, dry, aromatic white, with a distinct but not painful acid edge, will rise to the occasion.

4

STARTERS

Nothing succeeds like a good starter. Main courses may be the high point of a meal, and a dessert the reward for having consumed all your essential nutrients, but the dish with which anything from a modest lunch to a grand dinner begins often has a peculiarly satisfying quality all of its own. The reason for this is not difficult to see. It is that, if we are sitting down to eat in the state that nature intended, this is when we are at our hungriest, and the impact that the opening course makes on both palate and stomach is an especially enjoyable one.

For much the same reason, choosing a wine to go with the first course probably requires more precision and delicate judgment than does the wine for any of the succeeding dishes. A mismatch is certainly less forgivable at this stage than later on (unless it be the serving of dry champagne with a dessert, of which more in Chapter 10).

We are also confirmed enemies of the habit of serving only one wine with a multi-course meal, and not just because we like a drink. Although ordering two bottles can often be prohibitively expensive (and may well be far too much wine anyway, if there are only two of you), ordering one only could well leave you with a nice, sturdy claret that's fine with the red-meat main courses, but which will

murder the shellfish starters. This used to be the bugbear
of eating out in the kinds of restaurants where the wine
mark-ups assume you will have remortgaged your house
before making the booking. The solution to this is increasingly apparent in those lists that offer a fair selection – and
not just the house wines – by the glass. Have a glass of
something light and apposite with the first course, and
then a bottle, or a couple of glasses, of something else to
accompany the main. If only the glass mark-ups themselves weren't so punishing . . .

At home, these hard financial considerations are much
softened, and any wine that doesn't get finished over
dinner can be recorked and enjoyed the next day. So
choose a wine to go with the starter. If you've put just as
much effort into it as into the main course, after all, it
deserves its own moment in the gastronomic spotlight.

The most perfect succession of wines at a meal is a
serene progression from a sparkling (or dry fortified)
aperitif through a dry white and on to a red and, with that
in mind, the majority of recommendations in this chapter
are for a white wine. But we are not sticklers for tradition
for its own sake, and there are cases where a light red, or
even a sweet or off-dry white, are appropriate for an hors
d'oeuvre. These have found their way into our suggestions
too. Where fish, such as smoked salmon or marinated
herrings, is traditionally served as a first course, we have
included it here. Otherwise, look to Chapter 5 for our main
fish and shellfish recommendations.

Asparagus There is simply no better grape variety for
matching with asparagus than Sauvignon Blanc. The pungent, often slightly vegetal nature of the wine is perfect
with the earthy flavour of the vegetable. With plain
steamed asparagus, dressed with nothing more than a little
melted butter, a full and fruity New Zealand Sauvignon is

best, owing to its roundness of texture. If you are serving a **hollandaise sauce** with it, higher acidity in the wine will help, in which case go for a French Sauvignon (Sancerre if the budget allows, a Pays d'Oc or Touraine Sauvignon if not), or else one from South Africa. Avoid any that have been oak-aged. They will overpower the food.

Avocado The fattiness of texture of avocado requires a wine with good acid bite to counteract it. A simple Sauvignon Blanc works, as does a good, fruity Chenin Blanc from South Africa. A youthful Riesling from Australia or New Zealand is also an option. If you are serving the avocado with **prawns**, go for something a little more opulent, such as a youthful Riesling from Australia or New Zealand. With **crab**, more richness is called for: a reasonably mature (i.e. at least two-year-old) Chablis is good.

Black and white puddings A starter of fried **black pudding** (or, if you are reading this in France, *boudin noir*) has become a fashionable restaurant dish of late. It often appears with a poached egg, bacon and saladings, like a rather late breakfast but, in any case, the two elements to be aware of here are spice and fat. Black pudding is really much better off with a light red wine than with a white. One of the sturdier wines of Beaujolais (such as Morgon or Moulin-à-Vent), Italian Barbera, Australian Tarrango or even one of the lighter Zinfandels of California would all work. For **white pudding**, which is much lighter in texture and less pungent in flavour, a white wine is better. A little vegetal pungency in the wine will not go amiss here: Sylvaner from Alsace or the Franken region of Germany, an old-fashioned Müller-Thurgau from New Zealand, or a Sauvignon or Chenin with a fair amount of herbaceousness in the flavour (South Africa, Chile) are good bets.

Brandade The famous Mediterranean dish of dried salt

cod, reconstituted and made into a gloriously creamy purée with milk and olive oil, calls for bone-dryness and high acidity. If in doubt, always try to choose a wine from the same region that the dish itself, or its main ingredient, comes from. In this case, a young Spanish or Portuguese white, vinified without oak, will be the star choice. Portuguese whites made from the Ferñao Pires variety will answer the call, as would a Spanish white from the northern Rueda region (which may well contain a proportion of Sauvignon in with the local Verdejo grape), or – rather more expensively – a Rias Baixas from Galicia. Brandade itself, though, is a Provençal dish, and one of the rarely seen white wines of Provence, such as Palette or Cassis (not to be confused with the black-currant liqueur of the same name) would be ideal.

Carpaccio Wafer-thin slices of air-dried beef, often garnished with shavings of Parmesan and dressed in olive oil, carpaccio is a surprisingly obliging dish for pairing with wine. As red meat, it may seem to mandate a red wine, but it doesn't insist on it. A full-flavoured, pointedly fruity white can work quite satisfactorily – unoaked or lightly oaked Chardonnays from Chile or New Zealand are good – and there are impeccably sound cultural reasons to go for a Tuscan white such as a Vernaccia di San Gimignano. If there is plenty of Parmesan with it, though, a red might seem safer, in which case choose either a lightish Tuscan, such as simple Chianti with a couple of years' bottle-age, or else Rosso di Montalcino, or perhaps a Sangiovese-based wine from Argentina or California.

Caviare The traditional Russian partner for caviare is best vodka – one of the classier, ultra-refined grades of neutrally flavoured vodka, served painfully cold in a shot-glass. It is hard to better this with any product of the grape, but one thing that almost never works is champagne. At least, a fairly mature vintage blanc de blancs champagne might just stand up to one of the more gently flavoured types of caviare, such as oscietra or the mind-blowingly expensive beluga, but with the deliciously intense, salty sevruga, it will be blown away. Champagne is a delicate wine. Its expensiveness won't save it in this context. Instead, choose a neutrally flavoured white, such as an unoaked Chardonnay or Pinot Grigio from almost anywhere, and serve it well-chilled. If the quality is good enough, traditional Italian whites based on the Trebbiano variety work well enough: Frascati, Orvieto or Soave Superiore. Strange but true. The point is the neutrality of flavour. If the little birthday or Christmas tin of black grains has cost a day's wages, after all, there's no point in killing it stone-dead with the wrong wine.

Charcuterie Cured pork products such as salami, garlic sausage, mortadella ham or any of the manifold charcuterie delicacies of France need wines with plenty of flavour and probably a fair amount of alcohol (upwards of 13%) to do them justice. Some go for a midweight red, such as a young Bordeaux, a Loire red such as Chinon, unoaked Spanish Rioja or Italy's Montepulciano d'Abruzzo, depending on the nationality of the meat but, as with most cold starters, a plate of charcuterie is possibly happier with a white wine. Cut the fattiness of the meats with Alsace or Californian Riesling, South African Chenin, unoaked Australian Semillon or, as a speciality, a northwest Italian Arneis.

Cured hams The speciality dried hams of Europe, such as Italy's Parma, Spain's Serrano, France's Bayonne and Germany's Westphalia, are all best with white wines that are not too acidic, but have distinct aromatic personality. Think Riesling (from Alsace, New Zealand or Australia), Alsace Pinot Gris, or even Gewürztraminer from California or Chile. A light Italian red, perhaps Barbera or Dolcetto, is preferred by some with Parma ham, but anything other than the most vestigial hint of tannin can interfere with your appreciation of the meat.

Deep-fried cheeses The appearance of an individual, crumb-coated piece of soft cheese (typically Camembert, sometimes Brie), served with a tangy relish usually made of red fruits, as a starter has become enough of an abiding feature of pub menus to wonder whether there is anything in the global vineyard to go with it. The cheese itself isn't the problem; it's that sweet, acidic relish. Best bet would be a light, high-acid, low-tannin red such as Italian Dolcetto, one of the lighter, cheaper Beaujolais (e.g. Brouilly) or Gamay varietal from elsewhere (such as California), or perhaps a Loire red such as Bourgueil or Chinon from a ripe vintage.

Deep-fried mushrooms Those little, breadcrumbed button mushrooms will take any kind of wine you care to throw at them, quite frankly. It's what's in the dip that makes the difference. A fairly bland **sour-cream-and-chive** dip needs a bland, medium-sharp white, such as an unoaked Chardonnay from wherever springs to mind first. A stronger **garlic mayonnaise** needs something a little sharper in terms of acidity: Spanish Verdejo, Italian Verdicchio, or one of the more abrasive whites of southern France, perhaps a Clairette du Languedoc of the latest vintage.

Egg dishes Eggy starters do pose problems for wine, but are by no means the minefield of popular myth. It's best to ignore the garnish in anything garnished with a poached egg, and match the wine to the main ingredient, but creamy **scrambled eggs with smoked salmon** is worth a wine to itself. And what it's worth is champagne, or some top-quality sparkling wine from California, South Africa, Australia or New Zealand. With smoked salmon alone (see below), sparkling wines come to grief, but when its piercingly smoky flavour and saltiness are mitigated by being enveloped in egg, it becomes an ingredient fit to show its face in the presence of a delicate fizzy wine. For **scrambled eggs with asparagus**, follow the asparagus-and-hollandaise guidelines above. **Scrambled eggs with shavings of black truffle** demand something altogether luxurious. Top-notch, oaked Chardonnay, whether from Burgundy, California, Chile, New Zealand, South Africa or Australia will all do the dish proud. A dish in which the egg is fried, such as a French **omelette** or **pipérade**, Spanish **tortilla** or Italian **frittata**, will also need a correspondingly richer, more buttery wine. A lightly oaked Chardonnay or Semillon from Australia, Alsace Pinot Gris or a mid-priced white burgundy such as Montagny or Rully will do the trick. Meaty ingredients, such as chunks of sausage or smoked ham, might incline you towards a light red, such as a young unoaked Rioja or Navarra, or one of the lighter Languedoc reds such as Faugères or Fitou.

Goats' cheese Much as with asparagus, there is one wine that goats' cheese likes to snuggle up with more than any other, and once again, it's Sauvignon Blanc. It scarcely matters what the preparation is either. It can be served as it is with some salad leaves, or lightly baked or 'toasted', so that it has just begun to melt within (a slice of goats' cheese atop a short-pastry tartlet of caramelised onions has been a restaurant stalwart of latter times): it still works best with Sauvignon. The very best Sauvignon to serve with mature French chèvre, such as Crottin de Chavignol, is Sancerre, the local wine. But Pouilly-Fumé is just as good, as are the lesser-known Loire Sauvignon appellations of Menetou-Salon, Quincy and Reuilly. The more tropically fruity the Sauvignon, the less precise a match it is, so some of those Marlborough examples from New Zealand's South Island may be as well giving place to the flinty, chalky styles of the Loire, South Africa or Hungary.

Gravad lax The Scandinavian dish of cured, unsmoked salmon with its mustard-and-dill dressing is traditionally drunk on its home turf with a glass of vigorously chilled aquavit. Despite the relative sweetness of the dressing, though, a white wine will come to no harm, especially if it has a little residual sweetness of its own. Alsace Gewürztraminer and Pinot Gris are good, as are the more robustly constituted off-dry Rieslings of Germany (those of the Rheingau, Pfalz or Nahe regions). Oaky Australian Chardonnays are fine with this dish, as is mature *premier* or *grand cru* Chablis, if you're really pushing the boat out.

Hummus An earthily aromatic white wine, with a fair degree of youthful acidity and no oak, is what the Greek purée of chickpeas, tahini, oil, lemon and garlic needs. Spread on pitta bread, and accompanied by one of the new generation of Greek white wines, such as Assyrtiko or Robola, this is a heavenly lunch starter for a hot day. If the new generation of Greek white wines hasn't reached your locale yet, go for any young southern European white. Bulgarian Chardonnay comes from the right corner of Europe. Better might be one of Italy's whites, such as Verdicchio dei Castelli di Jesi, Orvieto Classico or Bianco di Custoza.

Italian antipasti Where you are presented simply with a plate of cooked meats, it is as well to follow the guidelines for cured ham above. Antipasti platters can be much more complex and various than this, however, incorporating mushrooms, black and green olives, artichoke hearts and other marinated vegetables, and even lemon-dressed shellfish as well. All this makes for something of a challenge. An astringent, high-acid white wine, well-chilled, is probably the best compromise. Young Riesling from New Zealand or Australia, Pays d'Oc Viognier of the latest vintage, or one of the lighter white blends of the Torres winery in Penedés, such as Viña Sol or Gran Viña Sol, are all good. An Italian choice is only proper though: young Chardonnay from Trentino or Alto-Adige, Tocai-Friulano or Traminer from the northeast, or Albana di Romagna will all work a treat.

Lobster Served cold in a salad with mayonnaise, lobster is happiest with a surprisingly light white that doesn't interfere with its singular flavour. *Premier cru* Chablis, or other cool-climate quality unoaked Chardonnay, is a sympathetic partner.

Marinated herrings As with gravad lax, a shot of stone-cold aquavit sounds the right Baltic note with firm-textured herrings. If dressed with a sharp vinaigrette and some chopped onion, a fresh young Sauvignon or Riesling are best, anywhere from Sancerre to Chile in the former case, from Alsace to New Zealand in the latter. Those jars of marinated rollmops in dressings that may comprise ketchup or mustard, and are nearly always acutely sweet, are best avoided on a gastronomic occasion.

Melon No great friend of any table wine, melon is best served either with a glass of chilled Sercial or Verdelho madeira, a tot of pale cream sherry, or – best of all – a small glass of ginger wine (some of which can be poured into the hollow of a halved small melon), as long as it isn't being served with Parma ham. If it is, stick with one of those fortified wines.

Oysters The bracing, salty tang of oysters served fresh in the shells with just a squeeze of lemon, and perhaps a few drops of Tabasco, makes a good background for a relatively neutral, high-acid white. Muscadet is a very traditional partner to oysters in Brittany. Chablis too is an appetising match. Both should be served very cold. One of the unoaked whites of southern Burgundy, such as St-Véran, will come to no harm, and there are some who can drink one of the fruitier Loire Sauvignons with them. Try Sancerre. Otherwise, a well-chilled, non-vintage blanc de blancs champagne, or some other predominantly Chardonnay fizz, is OK. The oysters are strongly flavoured, but then as they only spend such a very short time in the mouth, they won't do too much damage to a light sparkler.

Pasta dishes It always makes us laugh to see wine labels that say 'good with pasta', as though the object of the exercise was to match the pasta itself, rather than what goes with it. There are many different recipes of course, but the following four are the most frequently encountered. **Tomato-based sauces** need a vigorous young Italian red. Chianti, Rosso di Montalcino, Montepulciano d'Abruzzo, Barbera, and Trentino reds from such lesser-known grapes as Teroldego, are the business; their acidity stands up well to the acid bite of tomato. With **creamy sauces** such as carbonara, containing ham, a richly oaked white is best. Here, it pays to depart from Italy, and go perhaps to one of the Reserve Chardonnays of California, Chile, Australia or New Zealand. **Bolognese**, a sturdy sauce using minced beef, is best with one of the bigger reds of Italy. Salice Salentino or a Negroamaro-based blend from Puglia in the southeast are good, as is Aglianico del Vulture from Basilicata, or the more simple Sangiovese di Romagna. Wines made from Italian varieties in other countries are worth trying out too. Pasta **with seafood** needs one of the lighter whites, nothing oaky or too fruity, but young, cold and refreshing. Soave (from the Veneto), Frascati (Lazio), Orvieto (Umbria) and Gavi (Piedmont) are all traditional Italian accompaniments. Otherwise, branch out into the cooler regions of the southern hemisphere – Chile's Casablanca, Tasmania, New Zealand's Marlborough – for unoaked, or lightly oaked, Chardonnays.

Pâtés and terrines These ever-popular first-course dishes call for white wines rather than red, even where they involve red meats, such as duck liver pâté or a game terrine. Alsace and Germany are the best sources of these, with Pinot Gris, Gewürztraminer, Pinot Blanc and Riesling the most fitting varieties for the meatier types, such as chicken or duck liver,

game or pâté de foie gras, which last is best of all with a
Gewürztraminer that has distinct, but not overwhelming,
residual sweetness. Many people regard the marriage of
Sauternes and foie gras as made in heaven. Your authors,
alas, are a house divided on this issue, and leave it to your
own best judgment. With fish pâtés and terrines, a lighter
white may well be called for, unless the fish is smoked
(salmon, trout or mackerel), in which case, a lightly oaky
Chardonnay from somewhere, or perhaps a lightly oaky
Viura from the north of Spain, are fine. With pâtés of tuna
or crab, where a richness of both flavour and texture
demand an answering degree of substance in the wine, go
for a white with big alcohol. Australian Semillon will come
into its own here.

Salads The number of classic salad recipes is legion.
They don't always have to be compositions of ingredients
on a bed of leaves (some don't involve leaves at all), but
what we are talking about here are first-course dishes,
rather than accompaniments to main courses, or palate-
refreshers before the cheese or dessert. A pile of **rocket
leaves**, adorned with Parmesan and as often as not dressed
in olive oil and balsamic vinegar, is an austere modern
treat, and best paired with a herbaceous white such as dry
Chenin (Vouvray from the Loire) or Sauvignon (perhaps
one of the softer ones from California). A **seafood salad**
should be served with a well-chilled, acid-edged white of
the Muscadet or Chablis (or other unoaked Chardonnay)
type. A salad containing **artichoke** plays merry hell with
wine, as the bitterness of the vegetable makes most wines
seem curiously sweeter than they really are. Go for the
driest, then, such as young Australian or Alsace Riesling,
or the increasingly better-known Grüner Veltliner of
Austria. That fashionable French gastronomic salad of
Roquefort and walnuts, often including wedges of ripe
pear, is best with a sweet wine, to counteract the salty

richness of the cheese. A small glass of Sauternes, or Vendange Tardive Alsace, or late-picked Muscat from Australia or California, are all good. Drink a high-acid Italian white – Verdicchio or young Frascati – with that 1980s favourite, **mozzarella, tomato and basil**. A **Greek salad** needs either a Greek white (but not retsina!), or one of the fresh young whites made from indigenous varieties in Spain or Portugal (Portuguese Roupeiro is a fine match, if you can find one). **Caesar salad**, with its creamy, garlicky dressing and grated Parmesan, will stand up to a ripely tropical Chardonnay or Viognier from outside Europe (California, New Zealand or Chile being the favourites). The tuna and egg in **salade niçoise** call for a fairly big white made without oak, such as a white Côtes du Rhône, the white version of central Portugal's Dão, or even a rosé such as Côtes de Provence. **Waldorf salad** is best with something a touch off-dry, such as a demi-sec Vouvray or basic German blend.

Savoury soufflés The time and effort that soufflés require mean that they should be served with rather grand wines, even though their airy lightness may suggest otherwise. With a soufflé made of **white fish**, a classically balanced Chardonnay without too much oak is a sumptuous match. The balance of lightly honeyed fruit and lemony acids in fine white burgundy, including Chablis (ideally a *premier cru*) are better than the heavier styles made in the hotter regions. A **cheese** soufflé unequivocally needs a red wine to go with it: almost any midweight red with restrained tannins will serve, whether it be from the southern Rhône, Spanish Tempranillo, Italian Barbera or Sangiovese, Merlot from Chile, Washington State, eastern Europe, etc.

Savoury tarts and quiches The egginess of traditional quiche, perhaps further enriched with cheese, calls for a richly constituted white. Pinot Gris from Alsace or

Oregon, Semillon from Australia or California, and barrel-aged Chardonnay are all great partners for **quiche lorraine**. Anything made with **mushrooms** and served hot will take a lightish red, such as Chinon from the Loire, a Tempranillo-based blend from Rioja or Navarra, or blended Côtes du Rhône. The traditional French dish **flamiche**, most popularly made with leeks, will benefit from the grassy pungency of Loire Sauvignon.

Scallops Probably the most popular shellfish starter on restaurant menus these days, scallops have become something of a chameleon dish, appearing in as many different preparations as chicken does. That is largely because their flavour is so obligingly delicate, its chief characteristic being a kind of soft sweetness, to offset which they are often paired with sharply acidic accompaniments. Simply **grilled**, or briefly 'seared' in hot oil in the modern way, they are best with a lightish white with just a touch of residual sweetness. German Rieslings of the Kabinett or Spätlese categories, Alsace Pinot Blanc or Pinot Gris or, at a pinch, one of the hot-climate Chardonnays (from Chile or Australia, say) work well. With sharp **vinaigrettes**, or prepared in the **ceviche** fashion (with a scything citrus marinade and onion), they can take something with a little more edge: think New Zealand Sauvignon Blanc, Australian or New Zealand Riesling, Californian Chenin Blanc or good Muscadet de Sèvre-et-Maine *sur lie*. Served in a **creamy or cheesy sauce** in the old-fashioned way, a richer, moderately oaky Chardonnay or Semillon will do them proud. Oaky white Bordeaux from the Pessac-Léognan district, Australian Semillon or – perhaps best of all – a gently oaky white burgundy, such as Santenay, Rully or Pouilly-Fuissé, will all fit the bill.

Seafood cocktails The oily pink dressing on classic prawn or crab cocktail is a bit hard on wine. This really is one of those occasions for keeping it simple and inexpensive. Unoaked whites with keen acidity are best: Muscadet, Frascati, Touraine Sauvignon, dry Chenin from Vouvray or South Africa, etc.

Shrimps Potted shrimps, such as the inestimable ones from Morecambe Bay in the northwest of England, are buttery and grand enough to cope with a rich, buttery Chablis, even one of *grand cru* status. Otherwise, go for a similar style of Chardonnay from Chile, New Zealand or the United States.

Smoked fish (salmon, trout, mackerel, kippers, Arbroath smokies) Here again, we must enter a plea on behalf of champagne. Don't. With a fillet of **smoked trout**, it will just about do, but **smoked salmon** absolutely kills it. The oiliness, smokiness and saltiness need something much sturdier. Splash out on a premium oaked Chardonnay from Burgundy (Meursault is good), the United States or the southern hemisphere, or go for a big, strapping Viognier (Condrieu or best Californian if the bank balance will support such extravagance, pays d'Oc, Chile or central Europe if wiser counsels prevail). **Smoked mackerel** is better with something a little more down-to-earth, with Sauvignon, Riesling, Austrian Grüner Veltliner and Spanish Viura leading the charge. A warm **kipper** as a starter needs a surprisingly delicate white (a smokily oaked Chardonnay will be just too much of a good thing). Try a southern French blend, such as Coteaux du Languedoc or white Corbières, or that old Italian standby, Soave (but buy one labelled Classico, from the best part of the region). Scotland's other speciality, the **Arbroath smokie**, a dried fillet of smoked haddock, needs much the same treatment, except that it will forgive a little oak in the wine.

Snails with garlic butter This canonical Burgundian speciality needs a light red to go with it. Burgundy itself is inevitably perfect, the acidity of the Pinot Noir grape cutting through the copious quantities of butter, but don't go mad. A simple Bourgogne Rouge, or Côtes de Beaune-Villages, will do quite well. Italian reds work quite well too. Try Chianti or Barbera.

Soups Once we have established the general rule that most soups are really better off taken just as they are, without an accompanying wine, since a match of liquid with liquid is not the smartest idea, there are certainly no taste problems arising between most soups and a glass of wine (except for tomato soup, which really won't be satisfied). Keep it light, bland and white for most **vegetable-based cream soups**, a little richer for a creamy **chicken soup**, go for a light red or rosé with **oxtail**, and a light Italian red with **minestrone**. A modest tot of one of the drier brown fortified wines, such as amontillado sherry or Sercial or Verdelho madeira, is a classic and successful partner for a **consommé**, and also works well with **French onion soup**. Fishy soups such as **bouillabaisse** or the traditional **Provençal fish soup**, served with grated cheese, rouille and croûtons, will take a richer white, perhaps even one with a little oak, while creamy, alcohol-rich **bisques** of lobster or crab can cope with a richer one still. Bone-dry fino and manzanilla sherry each make an impeccable match with chilled Spanish **gazpacho**. Choose a fruity Sauvignon, or else a decent Muscadet de Sèvre-et-Maine *sur lie*, to go with the fieriness of **hot-and-sour Thai soup**. Drink concentrated Californian or Washington reds or whites with chunky, southern-style **chowders**, depending on whether the principal ingredients are meat or fish.

Tapas The immense variety of these little Spanish appetisers, which may take in eggs, potatoes, cheese, olives, seafood and *morcilla* (Spain's answer to black pudding), is too broad to make any one wine a comprehensive match. As long as it's Spanish, you're probably doing the right thing, and we have a hunch that sturdy whites are probably better than reds. Best of all, though, is to drink impeccably chilled manzanilla or fino sherry, just as if it were a regular white table wine. It really does have the versatility to cope.

Taramasalata This oily, garlicky Greek fish purée, which should be made with the roe of the grey mullet according to the textbook but is usually cod these days, demands a white wine with enough acidity to counterbalance its texture. New Zealand Sauvignon, Australian Riesling and South African Chenin are all good bets, as of course is any Greek white you can lay hands on (even the little-liked retsina). The alternative route is youthful rosé, from the south of France, Spain or Argentina, which has the combined weight and freshness to match.

5

FISH, SHELLFISH AND CRUSTACEANS

There is a tendency abroad these days to suggest that the business of matching wine and food all grew much too technical at some indeterminate time in the recent past, and that the best solution to these matters is to please yourself and drink whatever lies to hand, whether it be Soave or Valpolicella, Syrah or Viognier, lukewarm root beer or watermelon-flavoured Bacardi Breezer. It may fairly be assumed on the part of the reader that we are not of this party, otherwise we should scarcely be spending our time compiling a book of advice on the subject. There is much flexibility within the field, of course, but it is also possible to stretch the elastic to snapping point, and with the exception of desserts, there is no food category in which greater care is needed in choosing the wine than with fish dishes.

'Most wines go with most dishes,' runs this latest wisdom, which makes a tempting enough and easily memorable dictum, but is also vague to the point of prevarication, and permits of sufficient exceptions to make the two 'mosts' in it distinctly misleading. Nor is it simply a question of remembering that most red wine does not go with most fish, which it emphatically doesn't, but also that it is quite easy to overburden the flavour of a simply prepared delicate white fish such as sole or John Dory with too heavy a white wine. Quite as important as the flavours of a wine in this regard is its *weight* – the body and texture of it – on the palate. Only the firmest-textured fish, such as monkfish or snapper, together with the likes of lobster and the brown meat of crab, are likely to stand up to a strongly constituted wine.

For these reasons, the great majority of the wines recommended in this chapter will be dry white wines of one sort or another, but within that general rubric, there is still plenty of room for manoeuvre. Remember that once you have established the basic principle of a match – that is, which particular style of wine goes with which particular dish – you can always ring the changes on similar styles of wine from all over the known world. You will doubtless come up with successful combinations that we ourselves have not yet dreamed of.

And most of them will no doubt be considerably more convincing than the youthful red burgundy we were enjoined to drink with a buttery-sauced fillet of sea bass at a recent lunch. The encouragement to try red wines with white fish has almost attained the tenor of a government propaganda campaign in some quarters. With certain exceptions, detailed in the recommendations that follow, there is almost invariably no point in trying this experiment. Ridiculous mismatches of particular wines with food are more often than not urged on us by winemakers, or their commercial representatives, because they would like to see their products receiving a greater share of market action. (That was the case with that silly sea-bass-and-burgundy pairing, incidentally.) A winemaker in the Rheingau region of Germany once tried to convince us that his undoubtedly well-made, but featherlight, Rieslings would be a good match for roast lamb. And in Champagne, they are forever coming up with preposterous gastronomic suggestions, largely because champagne, as the most artificially contrived style of wine made anywhere in France, doesn't have obvious table partners, in the sense that the wines of other regions go symbiotically with those regions' traditional cuisines.

So be gentle with fish. It never did you any harm after all and, these days, it is usually of a price – in the supermarkets and inland fishmongers, at any rate – to make it worth getting the wine match right.

Remember also that, as with meat dishes, what matters at least as much as the character of the main ingredient is the method by which it is prepared. A rich, heavy, or tangily acidic sauce or dressing can fundamentally alter, or throw into relief, the flavours of a piece of fish. Indeed, that is its main function. As well as that, there are the other supporting ingredients, and even the seasoning, to consider: aromatic herbs and spices may also play their part in the range of tastes in a complex fish dish. We have covered some of the classic fish preparations in this chapter, but haven't forgotten that the simpler treatments also work best for many people. What could be better than a piece of impeccably fresh fish, simply grilled or baked, and served with nothing more than melted butter and a squeeze of lemon?

Brill This firm-fleshed flatfish, similar in texture and appearance to the turbot, is generally compared unfavourably with it. It's true that it isn't overendowed with character, but it is still worth a punt every now and then, and it does crop up regularly on restaurant menus. One of the traditional ways of cooking it in the south of France and northern Spain is **with cider**, in which case you might like to drink a dry French *cidre* or Spanish *sidra* (yes, they do exist) with it. Then again, you might not, and in its place, we suggest a dry, delicate white – something like a Rueda or Rias Baixas from northwest Spain, or a fairly bland southern French white such as white Côtes du Rhône. In the Basque region, brill is cooked **with peppers and onions**, in which case you should go for something a little more aromatic, such as a Loire or Spanish Sauvignon Blanc or New Zealand Riesling. If the fish is to be simply grilled, keep the wine as neutral as possible. An unoaked Chardonnay (Chablis, for example) or a Soave will do.

Cod When straightforwardly **fried or grilled**, cod will respond well to gentle dry whites without too much oak. Go for the lighter burgundies, such as Chablis, Montagny and Rully, unoaked Australian Chardonnays, Pinot Blanc from Alsace or Italian Pinot Grigio. The fashion now is to give it a fairly robust treatment, with rich (often meat stock-based) sauces, wild mushrooms, truffled mash, the works. One of us has even eaten a piece of cod with a Parmesan crisp stuck in the top of it, and lived to tell the tale. For these richer treatments, go with a correspondingly richer white – an oakier Burgundian Chardonnay such as Pouilly-Fuissé or Meursault, or one from California, Chile or Australia, or perhaps a distinguished *cru classé* white Bordeaux from the Graves district.

Crab A whole **dressed crab with salad** needs a fittingly grand wine to go with it. The problem with it is that the brown and white meats offer quite different flavours – the former rich and seafoody, the latter quite bracing but bland. It is possible to drink a light red with the brown meat (such as a Brouilly from Beaujolais), but an opulent, well-built white with oak is undoubtedly better, and shouldn't overwhelm the white meat too much. Viognier, whether from Condrieu in the Rhône, the pays d'Oc, California or Chile, is a very sympathetic match. If you like the white meat only, go with a lighter white, but a quality one still. German Riesling of Kabinett or Spätlese class is fine, as is the unoaked Semillon of the Hunter Valley, Australia.

Dover sole This fish seems to have fallen from favour in the pace-setting restaurants in recent years, which is a shame because it is a noble beast, very light in texture and delicate in flavour, but lending itself to a number of alluring recipes. **Plain-grilled** and squeezed with lemon, it needs a gentle unoaked Chardonnay, classically a Chablis, or Sauvignon Blanc from Chile or Hungary. If it has a **cream sauce**, up the quality of that Chablis to *premier* or *grand cru*, or go for one of the Reserve bottlings of Californian or Chilean Chardonnay. Those long, pliable fillets are good for wrapping round some form of stuffing in the *paupiette* fashion: if filled with **mushrooms**, choose a rich, earthy white, such as Alsace Pinot Gris or Austrian Grüner Veltliner; if filled with **smoked salmon**, make it a Gewürztraminer from Chile, New Zealand or Germany. An old favourite bistro dish, *sole véronique*, in which the fish is cooked with sweet green grapes, is excellent with a dry Muscat, pre-eminently one from Alsace.

Eel A highly popular fish in Spain and Portugal, eel is very firm and meaty, and is one of those fish that will happily take a red wine. Cut up in chunks and served in what the Portuguese call a *caldeirada*, a sort of tomatoey **stew**, it works well with midweight Portuguese reds such as Dão and Bairrada, as well as Spanish reds like Valdepeñas. **Smoked eel** served as a main course, perhaps with a verdantly tangy *salsa verde*, is better with a smokily pungent white such as New Zealand Sauvignon Blanc, Sancerre, Pouilly-Fumé or good white Bordeaux.

Fish and chips You might think a can of export lager would be a good match for this erstwhile British national dish, especially as the natives so often eat it late at night on the way home from the pub, but beer is hardly ever a good match with fish. Good, fresh fish that hasn't been frozen, carefully prepared with a home-made batter – and keeping a sparing hand with the malt vinegar – deserves a nice glass of wine. Ordinary Chardonnay of the most recent vintage, fresh and lemony, or else an Italian Pinot Grigio or Soave, are all it asks.

Fish pie The classic English recipe for a fish pie involves a white fish like cod, together with smoked haddock and prawns, in a creamy béchamel-type sauce, under a blanket of mashed potato. It is a superbly comforting winter dish and, although simple in conception, is actually quite time-consuming to prepare, and rich to taste. It needs a full-bodied, buttery white wine. Ring the changes from barrel-aged Australian Semillon, Alsace Pinot Gris, white Rioja Crianza or wines of similar weight, or go with the flow and plump for a fine, cask-fermented Chardonnay from Chile, New Zealand, California, the pays d'Oc or Burgundy.

Haddock Haddock, like cod, is a relatively gently flavoured fish, and should not be drowned with an over-assertive wine. **Grilled or steamed**, it is best with a neutral dry white with a certain amount of acid bite (Muscadet or cool-climate unoaked Chardonnay are fine). **Battered**, it can take something a bit more aromatic, such as a dry Vouvray from the Loire, or Entre-deux-Mers from Bordeaux. Good undyed **smoked haddock** makes a wonderful main-course dish, often complemented these days by a **buttery hollandaise-type sauce** and/or a poached egg. Served this way, it will welcome the richest, oakiest styles of Chardonnay, from Australia, California and Burgundy. Simply **grilled or poached in milk**, and perhaps served with some new potatoes and wilted spinach, a lighter, more biting style of white is better. Think Riesling, Chenin or Sauvignon Blanc, from Alsace, the Loire or South Africa respectively.

Hake This very firm-textured Atlantic and Mediterranean fish is much appreciated on the Iberian peninsula, where they have a number of traditional preparations for it. It can take a lightish red if **stewed** with peppers and tomatoes. Portuguese Dão or Alentejo reds, Spanish Rioja Joven or Valdepeñas, or even a simple Pinot Noir from Italy, Spain or the Côte Chalonnaise region of Burgundy (e.g. Mercurey) are all good. If served with a fresh *salsa verde*, with plenty of parsley and other herbs, it is better off with a white, but go for a big one. Rioja Reserva or Portugal's Bucelas will answer the call.

Halibut Particularly prized for its combination of firmness without dryness, and good positive flavour, halibut is a true gastronomic fish. Served **grilled or poached**, it needs a brightly flavoured, but not overwhelmingly oaky, white: unoaked Australian Chardonnay, Californian Viognier, Chilean Sauvignon Blanc and Rieslings from Alsace or New Zealand will all, in their various ways, match it. With a **hollandaise sauce** and perhaps a little spinach, it can take something a sight richer. Go for more oak on that Chardonnay, or more bottle-age in the Riesling.

John Dory A fine, but lightly flavoured fish known to the Europeans as St Peter's fish, John Dory is best prepared as simply as possible. The fillets can be **fried or grilled**, in which case serve them with an opulent Burgundian Chardonnay or, for a change, a wine made from one of the lesser-known European varieties grown in Australia (Verdelho or Marsanne), or perhaps a Pinot Gris from Oregon or Washington State. If gently **poached**, go for a lighter style – perhaps a Chilean Sauvignon Blanc.

Kedgeree The famous old English dish of buttery rice with smoked haddock, hard-boiled egg and Indian spices requires a rich, smoky-flavoured white wine to cope with it. White Rioja Reserva, oak-aged Bordeaux from the Pessac-Léognan district, or any barrel-fermented Chardonnay from the likes of Chile, Australia, the south of France, Burgundy or California will all serve. Alternatively, try cutting the buttery richness of the dish with a razor-sharp Sauvignon Blanc from the Loire.

Lemon sole Long thought of as the poor relation of Dover sole, lemon sole is unfairly maligned. It is a delicate, but agreeably textured, fish that makes a perfect lunch dish. **Grilled or fried**, serve a light Italian white with it (Frascati, Orvieto, Alto-Adige Chardonnay). If served with a **creamy, lemony sauce**, choose something with a little more acidity, perhaps an Alsace or German Trocken (dry) Riesling, or a Chenin Blanc from South Africa.

Lobster A **cold lobster salad** with mayonnaise is a show-stopping main course, which deserves a very fine white to accompany it. *Premier cru* or *grand cru* Chablis, or some other premium unoaked Chardonnay from South Africa, California or Australia, would all set the right tone. It's also not bad with rosé: a southern French one from Tavel or Corbières, or one of the riper Cabernet Sauvignon rosés of Chile or Argentina. Served hot in that *haute cuisine* classic, **lobster thermidor**, it needs an oakier, fatter-textured wine, such as top Meursault or Puligny-Montrachet from Burgundy, or the best Californian Chardonnay that the available money can buy.

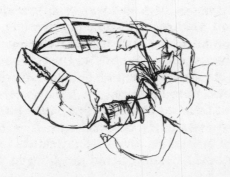

Monkfish One of the few fish that will go with either red or white wine, depending on the recipe, monkfish is a very meaty-textured fish with a lot of flavour. The tail end is a little gentler than the laterally cut steaks, but still needs a big wine. If it is served **roasted or fried**, and left fairly plain, it will benefit from a big, alcoholic white, such as the white versions of Hermitage or Châteauneuf-du-Pape from the Rhône, or a hefty Australian Semillon. In one of the meatier dishes commonly met with, perhaps **stewed in red wine** with bacon and onions or **wrapped in Parma ham or pancetta**, a rich red with a dollop of freshening acidity is called for. Try Barbera from Piedmont, Rosso di Montalcino or Montepulciano d'Abruzzo from central Italy, or a Pinot Noir from Italy, California, New Zealand or Chile.

Paella There are probably as many recipes for paella as there are inhabitants of Valencia, where the dish originated. In some versions, it isn't really a fish dish at all, containing only meat, but it is most commonly made with a mixture of **shellfish and white meat**, usually prawns, langoustines and mussels with chicken or maybe rabbit, all cooked with saffron-scented rice and olive oil. As such, it will go with red, white or pink wine, as the mood takes you, but with red the third choice. Best Spanish choices are the rosados or dry whites of Penedés, Rioja or Navarra, or the smaller regions of Calatayud or Conca de Barbera. Even a good vintage cava, Spain's sparkling wine, will marry quite well with it. Otherwise, Italian wines are the next best bet. Choose lightish reds such as Teroldego Rotaliano or Veneto Merlot, or aromatic whites like Arneis or Gavi from Piedmont.

Plaice An appealing flatfish with a subtle flavour, plaice needs a correspondingly discreet wine. It is best served either **grilled or fried** briefly in a light batter. Light whites such as South African Chenin or Chilean Sauvignon

Blanc, or one of the rare Sylvaners of Alsace, are good, or else go down the tried-and-true unoaked Chardonnay route, from the south of France, Chile or Australia.

Red mullet This very attractive, pink-skinned fish has been universally fashionable since the late 1980s, before which it was essentially a Mediterranean speciality. Best **grilled** with the skin left on, so that it puffs up and crisps, red mullet has plenty of flavour, and responds well to sharp, olive oil-based dressings. Serve it with Spanish and Portuguese whites, or with one of the rarely seen Greek white table wines (i.e. not the dreaded retsina). Otherwise, it's good with Sauvignon Blanc and Riesling from California, Viognier from Chile or South African Sauvignon, or perhaps a Spanish Rioja rosado. It has become all the rage lately to serve it with meaty accompaniments such as chorizo or white beans in a meat stock stew, in which case it will just about take a light Spanish red, something like the younger, unoaked versions of Rioja.

Salmon Not only the king of fish, salmon is also remarkably versatile when paired with wine. Red wine fans, read on: the good news starts here. Light reds from the Pinot Noir or Gamay varieties (the former from New Zealand or the Côte de Beaune, the latter from Beaujolais or California) are fascinatingly good with it, and will benefit from being served slightly chilled in this context. If that seems like too much of a shock to the system, the white repertoire is even broader. Rich, oak-matured wines stand up to the dense texture of the fish, while grassy, acid-edged whites cut the oiliness. Nor does the method of cooking matter much. Lightly **poached** salmon will still take either red or white, although cold salmon is undoubtedly better with white. **Baked** with tarragon and dill, it will go well with an Italian Arneis or Argentinian Torrontes. Go for a red if it is to be served with a **mustard sauce**, white with anything **creamy**, such as hollandaise.

Salmon fishcakes Once bound with potato and parsley, salmon needs a lighter, simpler wine than it does when served on its own. An Italian Pinot Grigio, unoaked Spanish Viura, Alsace Pinot Blanc or any of the unoaked Chardonnays of Australia, eastern Europe or Chile will fit the bill.

Salmon trout The rosy-fleshed sea trout is similar in texture to salmon, hence its name, and can be drunk with the same kinds of wines.

Scampi Breaded, deep-fried scampi, squeezed with lemon and served with crisp thin chips, has long been one of the superior British pub dishes, for all that it has its origins in Italian *fritto misto*. The fish filling is langoustine tails, which have a lightly lobstery flavour, and need pairing with a pretty rich white wine. Tip-top burgundy, such as Meursault or Chassagne-Montrachet, will come to no harm. A more realistic financial alternative would be lightly oaked Oregon or Californian Chardonnay, Chablis, New Zealand Chardonnay or Riesling, or a Tuscan white with some personality, such as Vernaccia di San Gimignano. Be sparing with the tartare sauce, though: it will obliterate the subtleties in those expensive burgundies.

Sea bass So popular in recent years that world stocks of it are suddenly rather low, sea bass is a fine fish, firm-textured and with full, rounded flavour. If the fish is to be **grilled or baked**, drink a well-structured, aromatic white with it, such as Australian Sauvignon Blanc or Riesling, South African Sauvignon, Chilean or New Zealand Chardonnay or Californian Riesling. Among the Europeans, head towards the classic Loire Sauvignon wines of Sancerre or Pouilly-Fumé, or a German Spätlese Riesling, or a Grüner Veltliner from Austria. If **steamed** in the Chinese fashion with spring onions and ginger, the Rieslings and Sauvignons will come into their own over the others.

Sea bream The densely textured and amply flavoured sea bream is good with much the same sorts of wines as sea bass. It is best **poached**, although one Andalusian speciality is to **bake** it whole inside a dry swaddling of sea salt, in which case it is incomparable served with stone-cold fino or manzanilla sherry.

Skate The fish that doesn't need to be filleted, since it can be easily combed off its bone (cartilage, really) on the plate, skate is a generously flavoured treat among white fish. In its time-honoured manifestation, with **capers and brown butter**, it needs a pungent Sauvignon Blanc, one from South Africa, Touraine or the upper Loire (i.e. Sancerre or Pouilly-Fumé). With a **meat stock sauce and mash**, which is something of a modern reference dish, choose a heavier white, such as an oaky Chardonnay, Alsace Pinot Gris, Australian Semillon or white Rioja.

Snapper This tropical fish is a tough customer, as its aggressive name implies. If stewed with peppers and tomatoes, it will accommodate a young red, such as a Burgundian or Chilean Pinot Noir, or Tempranillo from Spain or Argentina. Otherwise, white wines to go for would be fairly neutral-tasting but well-built specimens like Côtes du Rhône blanc, or a Viura or Macabeo-Chardonnay blend from Spain.

Squid Here, the wine choice depends crucially on the method of preparation. If the squid is **fried in oil**, a neutral-tasting white with middling acidity is best. Chablis is a reasonable, though not perfect, match, as are many of the more edgy Italian whites, such as Frascati Superiore or Piedmont's Arneis. When the dish is cooked in the Spanish fashion, **stewed in its own jet-black ink** with tomatoes and red wine, it cries out for a red wine to partner it, and a surprisingly robust one at that. Squid's texture tends to be quite chewy, even when lightly cooked, so a fair amount of tannin and oak in the wine seem appropriate. Big reds from Navarra, Ribera del Duero, even Toro, all do the dish justice, as would the sturdier Pinot Noirs of California and Chile.

Swordfish A swordfish steak will take a burly red, such is its density and gaminess of flavour. Even a claret from one of the lighter vintages, with a few years' bottle-age, won't stun it. Better though are Merlots from Chile, California and Washington State, Sangiovese from Tuscany (e.g. Chianti Classico) or Spanish Tempranillo. Spanish and Argentinian rosados, or French rosés from the southern Rhône or Languedoc, make a diverting change. Whites should be simple but sturdy, such as white blends from the same areas of southern France as those rosés.

Trout A fish of delicate flavour and fragile flesh once cooked, trout needs a very gentle white so as not to outshout it. For plainly **grilled or baked** trout, bring out your Alsace Pinot Blanc, nutty Italian Chardonnays from Alto-Adige or Umbria, unoaked Viura from Spain, or the unoaked Chardonnays of eastern Europe. Oak and overt aromatics will not please it one bit. That famous old cookery-book favourite, **trout with almonds**, will stand up to something with a little more body, such as a Pinot Gris from Alsace or a white Rioja Crianza.

Tuna Red-fleshed tuna is the nearest that fish comes to being meat and, as such, will cope with midweight red wines. Pinot Noir, Gamay and young Tempranillo are all impressive with it. New Zealand and California are best for Pinot. Or try a Châteauneuf-du-Pape or other southern Rhône blend. These are the best matches if the tuna is briefly **seared or chargrilled**. If it is **stewed** in the southern European style with tomatoes, onions and peppers in red wine, you could look to an oakier red to go alongside it. Rioja Reserva is fine, as is the smoothly inviting style of Washington State Merlot or even inexpensive Australian

Shiraz. If you prefer a white, go for a tropically fruity Chardonnay from Australia, New Zealand, Chile or California.

Turbot A rightly prized flatfish with good flavour and firmish texture, turbot is like a superior version of the blander brill. The white flesh should not be overpowered by its wine partner, which needs to be gently acidic, rather neutral in flavour and devoid of oak, but of definite quality. If the fish is plainly **grilled or steamed**, a Chablis, light southern burgundy such as Rully or Montagny, unoaked Chardonnay from South Africa or Tasmania, or something like fine Alsace Pinot Blanc will all behave in its company. With a rich sauce of **white wine and cream**, it can bear a weightier wine. Gently oaky Chardonnay from California, Oregon, New Zealand or South Africa, or a southern French Viognier, would be appropriate.

Zander This white-fleshed river fish, sometimes known as pike-perch, has to be one of the most boring items on the menu. Its bland, woolly meat and lack of flavour only really call for the most turgidly neutral of white wines. German or New Zealand Müller-Thurgau wines would do, as would any of the water-pale Trebbiano-based whites of Italy.

6

MEAT (BIRDS)

We have chosen to divide our meat chapters between bipeds and quadrupeds, as this seems to be a more logical and helpful division than the usual white meat and red, which often leads to a certain amount of confusion when it comes to discussing game birds.

Meat, of all food categories, is the one that permits of the greatest flexibility in choosing wine. There are many dishes with which the wine partner proves happily adaptable, depending on whether you want to drink red or white. It very much depends on the method of preparation. Different cooking techniques open up different wine possibilities, as do factors such as herb and spice seasonings and sauces. A poached chicken breast will require a rather different sort of wine from that called for by a whole roast chicken. Similarly, a dish made gently aromatic with chopped tarragon leaves has a distinctly different personality from one that is full of fresh red chilli. These are all factors to bear in mind, and take us far beyond the old approach of simply matching a wine to the main ingredient, whatever guise it turned up in on the plate.

Some will say that a wine should be matched to the sauce rather than the meat. There is some logic in this, certainly, but it is a little too broad-brush for our liking. A sauce doesn't necessarily provide the dominant flavour in a dish after all. It may be no more than a light moistening presence, a subtle form of liquid seasoning for the principal item. During the high-water mark of nouvelle cuisine in the late 1980s, sauces were very much an indispensable component of a dish, and often provided the main excitement when they offered some off-the-wall (and quite frequently highly inapposite) flavour. Thus did we find ourselves eating piercingly flavoured raspberry sauces with the likes of duck or even lamb, while chicken was considered the shameless hussy of the meat repertoire, apparently prepared to be seen with virtually any escort, be it mango, banana or juniper. Thankfully, restaurant cooking has returned to a sense of equilibrium now, and sauces have receded back to where they classically were, playing a supporting role to the meat rather than competing shrilly with it for attention. Many dishes now are sauced with little more than the lightest smear of some herb-scented stock reduction, which gives the sommelier (i.e. you) more of a variegated wine palette to paint from.

In the suggestions below, we have headlined the various categories of poultry and game birds, and then listed the major cooking methods and some of the classic European dishes for each one. (The major ethnic cuisines, such as Chinese, Indian and Thai, are treated separately in Chapter 9.) Not only the culinary handling, but which part of the bird is being served, is of importance. The darker meat of chicken and turkey, for example, is more tender and flavourful than the drier, blander – but undoubtedly most popular – breast meat. It's also worth bearing in mind that the quality of meat is all. For British readers, we strongly recommend meat from those butchers who are members of the Q-Guild, whose meat is reared in the old-fashioned way and not under intensive farming conditions. It is bound to have better flavour and texture than the cheapest on offer in the high street. (Go to www.guildofqbutchers.co.uk on the internet to find one near to you.)

We hope to surprise and provoke with our wine suggestions in this section. The edible range extends from light pale meats to dark and gamey ones, and the wine repertoire is correspondingly broad. It is also sufficiently flexible that the same red wine might just as well serve whether you are roasting quail at home or choosing ostrich from an adventurous restaurant menu.

CHICKEN

The best kind of chicken is a free-range, corn-fed bird that has been allowed to age respectably before slaughter. These have by far the best flavour in every part of the meat, and their creamy yellow flesh marries beautifully with a whole range of additional flavours, such as tarragon, garlic, lemon – even black truffles if you're feeling rather grand. Battery birds tend to be blander in flavour and more pappy in texture. The meat of the thighs and drumsticks is about the best.

Barbecued chicken Crisp, sizzling chicken pieces done on the barbecue, the skin blackened in stripes, or else slathered in some spicy marinade, are more appealing to many than sausages and steaks. Drink red or white as you prefer, but red is probably more of a star with any barbecued meat. Keep them soft and gentle though: Chianti Classico, Rioja Crianza, Côtes du Rhône red, California or Washington State Merlot, Chilean Merlot, Pinot Noir from New Zealand, or burgundies such as Mercurey or Givry have the sort of weight required. With very spicy marinades, particularly those heavy on chilli or mustard, go with something a little peppery, such as a northern Rhône red (e.g. Crozes-Hermitage) or a midweight Californian Zinfandel. If you want to drink white, try southern French Viognier, or one of the multifarious smoky-scented oaked Chardonnays the world has to offer.

Chicken and mushroom pie A mixture of chicken chunks and sliced mushrooms in white sauce bound in thick flaky pastry is an English lunchtime dish of the old school, still much in evidence on the menus of country pubs. On balance, we'd go for a rich white with it, a buttery Chardonnay from Chile or Argentina, Australia or eastern Europe, or perhaps a Pinot Gris from Alsace, but buttery rather than fruity. For a red, which the mushrooms will help the pie to stand up to, choose something fairly gentle, perhaps a Grenache-based blend from the southern Rhône, Languedoc, Roussillon or northern Spain (where the grape name becomes Garnacha).

Chicken chasseur Literally 'hunter's chicken', this is a dish of sautéed chicken pieces coated in a sauce of mushrooms, shallots and tomatoes cooked in white wine. There is nothing particularly *haute cuisine* about it, but it won't shame a fairly grand wine. The fact that it is cooked in white wine suggests that a white would be the obvious choice for drinking with it, but it will uncomplainingly (and a touch more sympathetically) take a red instead. It is of course a French dish, and it would seem churlish not to look to that country first for a match. A young ripe burgundy is good, as it so often is with chicken: choose one from the Côte de Beaune, such as Beaune itself or Pommard for reds, or perhaps a white Santenay, or start lower down the price scale with red or white Côtes de Beaune-Villages. Extrapolating outwards, you might light on Pinot Noirs or Chardonnays from other countries. Best are California, Oregon or New Zealand for the former, Chile, California, South Africa or New Zealand for the latter.

Chicken Kiev The dish that took western Europe by

storm in the 1970s isn't really anything to do with genuine Ukrainian cuisine, any more than chicken tikka masala is authentically Indian. It remains, however, a firm favourite as a midweek supper dish, especially welcome on cold nights, when the pungently strong garlic butter that oozes forth from it when cut seems a particular treat. It's a white wine dish, and the wine it needs is a none too subtle one at that. High acidity will cut the richness of the butter and the breadcrumb coating. Cool-climate unoaked Chardonnay or Chenin Blanc are right: Chablis, New Zealand, Tasmania or the Casablanca region of Chile are good sources for the Chardonnays, coastal South Africa and the central Loire (e.g. Vouvray and Montlouis) for Chenin. Light dry white Bordeaux, or similar unoaked Semillon-Sauvignon blends from elsewhere, work almost as well.

Chicken with Parma ham and tomatoes This is the kind of chicken dish you expect to find on a traditional Italian trattoria menu, probably a breast of chicken on the bone, wrapped in Parma ham or pancetta, and thickly coated with a herb-infused tomato sauce involving oregano or basil. Tomatoey sauces can strip the subtleties out of wine, making it seem either too acidic or too sweet, depending on the wine. White wines are best avoided with this dish. As with other tomato-based Italian dishes, what it really needs is a midweight, youthful Italian red with a controlled but definite quotient of nippy acidity. Best grapes to go for are Sangiovese (as in Chianti or other Tuscan or central Italian blends), Barbera from Piedmont in the northwest, Negroamaro from Puglia (look for a wine called Copertino) or even one of the lighter Nebbiolos. Italian varietals from other countries, such as California's and Argentina's Sangiovese or Argentina's Bonarda, will obviously make the right noises too.

Coq au vin The classic Burgundian concoction of chicken

stewed on the bone with bacon, shallots, mushrooms, garlic and herbs in a flour-thickened red wine liquor, after a brief flaming with cognac, is one of the most comforting dishes in the world. Originating from Burgundy, it is naturally happiest with one of that region's red wines, and you can be as extravagant as you like. The mushrooms and bacon in the recipe enable it to hold its own with the sturdiest and meatiest appellations of the Côte de Nuits, such as Gevrey-Chambertin and Morey-St-Denis. A basic Bourgogne rouge, or something like Hautes Côtes de Beaune, won't disgrace it, but choose one from a good ripe vintage. Pinot Noirs from most other regions are very much second-best, especially if they have a lot of bright red fruit on them, which doesn't seem right. Oregon, in the Pacific Northwest of the USA, is probably the best alternative bet, followed by South Africa. Cru Beaujolais, from just to the south of Burgundy, is a good partner too: best are Morgon, Moulin-à-Vent and Côte de Brouilly (but not so much Brouilly itself). Red Rioja works perfectly well too, but the feeling that you aren't really entering into the spirit of the dish will be hard to ignore.

Coronation chicken This cold dish of cooked chicken bound in a savoury, Indian-spiced mayonnaise containing chopped apricot, created by cookery writer Constance Spry for the coronation of Queen Elizabeth II in June 1953, is a summer picnic favourite. It is of course a white wine dish, and one that marries precisely with the Viognier grape variety. A good southern French vin de pays d'Oc Viognier will do, but if the budget allows, a more high-rolling version from California or from Condrieu in the northern Rhône is even better. Avoid any that have been aged in oak. Other fruitily aromatic varietals with assertive acidity to cut through the mayonnaise work well, Sauvignon Blanc and Riesling foremost among them. Go to New Zealand, Chile or South Africa for these.

Poached chicken breast in cream sauce Absolutely the gentlest, least demanding way to serve chicken is to poach a boneless breast in white wine, perhaps with a few sliced mushrooms and a little garlic, and then finish it with thick cream to make an opulent sauce. The wine it needs should be equally rich, with a certain amount of barrel contact adding creaminess of texture to match that sauce. Top-notch cask-aged Chardonnays are best, whether from Burgundy, California, Chile, South Africa, New Zealand or Australia (just about anywhere, in fact), but other oaky wines will do almost as well. Semillon from Australia or Bordeaux, Marsanne from Australia and white Rioja are all great, and so – among the rich but unoaked – are Alsace Gewürztraminer and Pinot Gris.

Roast chicken A whole roast chicken is one of the finest Sunday lunch dishes of all, particularly when the bird is a free-range, corn-fed one flavoured with herbs and garlic. It doesn't mind a bit whether you drink a red or a white wine with it. With a richly garlicky, mustardy gravy, it's probably a little better off with a red wine than with a white, and the crispy bits of skin (not to mention the roast potatoes) are better set off with a gently tannic, midweight red of some class, than with even the richest white. Pinot Noir is once again the star match, with Burgundy, California, Oregon and Chile all providing very smart escorts. The Gamay grape of Beaujolais performs well in this context (try a Fleurie or a Chiroubles), and some of Austria's and Germany's lighter reds, from grapes such as Blaufränkisch or Dornfelder, come into their own. For whites, a big Semillon from Australia's Hunter Valley is a winner, as are the oakier whites of the Graves district of Bordeaux. Viognier's not bad, having the right weight, even if it is a little piercingly fruity, and nearly all of Alsace's varietals (except perhaps Riesling) work well. Best of all for whites is probably a mature (i.e. at least three-year-old) *premier cru* or *grand cru* Chablis. If it's an Alsace Riesling you happen to have to hand, try stuffing a lemon into the cavity of the chicken and then adding its cooked juices to the gravy.

Southern-fried chicken The deep-fried chicken portions in their peppery crumb coating popularised by chains such as KFC can be eaten with wine too, but beware of any strongly flavoured dips. Smoky barbecue sauce and vinegary mustard dips, and certainly tomato ketchup, are all pretty much anathema to wine. The chicken itself, though, is as happy to go with either red or white wine as is roast or barbecued chicken. Best keep it simple, in keeping with the food: straightforward Chardonnays or simple Spanish or Italian whites, or else gentle, softly textured reds such as inexpensive Australian Shiraz, Rhône reds, eastern European Merlot or Spanish red blends. The red wines of any of those bulk-producing Californian wine combines, whose names we shall forbear to mention, are probably best glugged down with southern-fried chicken.

DUCK

At one time, the wonderfully rich, dark meat of duck was only ever served *à l'orange*, after which fruity accompaniments sort of stuck with it (black cherries were another popular treatment). These are indeed charming enough dishes in themselves, but somewhat traduced the versatility of the bird. Whether plain-roasted in the English fashion, or cooked as confit in the southwest French, it is a splendid meat, the fat of which is the monounsaturated kind that is thought to be much better for cardiac health than pork fat or dairy fat.

Cassoulet The traditional stewed dish of southwest France comes in several versions, depending on which town happens to be making it. Named after the wide pot in which it is cooked, it should always consist at least of

chunks of sausage, haricot beans and pieces of confit
duck with goose fat and a top-layer of garlicky bread-
crumbs. The red wines of the Languedoc are its nearest
regional matches, principally Corbières, Minervois and
Fitou, but other reds of the vicinity, such as Coteaux du
Languedoc, Faugères, Costières de Nîmes, Cahors or
Cabardès, are also acceptable partners. The principle, in
other words, is a Grenache/Syrah-based blend, which may
well contain proportions to taste of varieties such as
Mourvèdre, Cinsault and Carignan. (Among the above-
named, the exception is Cahors, which is principally made
from Malbec. Cabardès will likely have some Cabernet
Sauvignon and Merlot in with the Grenache and Syrah as
well.) If you don't happen to have access to these wines in
your market, try any Syrah- or Grenache-based blend
from elsewhere. Australia and California have some fine
examples, as of course does Spain, which will all go
perfectly well with cassoulet. It is a very forgiving dish.
White wine? Er, no.

Duck à l'orange With its sweetly tangy sauce based on
Grand Marnier liqueur, orangey duck needs a white wine
with some noticeable sweetness of its own. Ripe Alsace
wines, including the late-picked Vendange Tardive versions, work well, but they do tend to match the sauce
rather than the meat itself. In Bordeaux, they quite often
drink a Sauternes with fruity duck – an acquired taste, but
by no means an incoherent one for those with the capacity
for a lot of sugar. Red wines tend to crash into this dish
with the sound (and taste) of crumpling metal.

Duck confit Served on its own, with perhaps a light meat
stock sauce, duck confit is best with a good, rich, mildly
tannic red, which echoes the crispness of the skin and the
fatty density of the meat. Southwest France is an impeccable choice again, as with cassoulet (Cahors, Minervois and
Corbières are all superb with it), but northern Spain is fine

too (good Rioja Crianza, Navarra and Ribera del Duero).
Australian Cabernet Sauvignon, Chilean Merlot, South
African Shiraz and Cabernets from eastern Europe are
also good matches.

Duck with cherries The black cherries served with this
duck recipe call for a ripely fruit-filled red with a hint of
sweetness around its edges. Californian Zinfandel is a
stunning match in this context, having that precise combination. Cru Beaujolais with plenty of ripe cherry fruit of
its own (Brouilly, St-Amour or Fleurie) is also a star. Some
Spanish reds with plenty of oak are good too, particularly
Ribera del Duero. White wines are workable but less good
here, although a demi-sec Vouvray isn't bad, and even a
racily fruity New Zealand Sauvignon has its charms,
provided it isn't too acidic.

Roast duck Simply roasted duck, without any tricksy or
fruity sauces, cries out for a well-built, muscular red with
some spicy overtones. Rhône Syrah (Côte-Rôtie, St-Joseph,
Crozes-Hermitage) is great, as is Australian Shiraz or
Shiraz-Cabernet. The drier Zinfandels of California are
wonderful with it, and so are the fruity southern Italian reds
of Puglia (such as Salice Salentino) and Sicily. Spain and
Portugal give good value (an Alentejo red blend from the
southeast of Portugal makes an exciting combination), and
the Merlots of Chile and California work well. Some sturdy
white wines, such as Alsace Pinot Gris or a Pessac-Léognan
from Bordeaux, can make admirable partners for roast
duck.

OTHER BIRDS
Goose There are devotees of drinking white wine with the
roast goose at Christmas, but we tend not to number
ourselves among them. In Germany, where goose is still
much more the festive bird than it tends to be in the
turkey-obsessed Anglophone countries, the habit makes

sense. Their red wines wouldn't be much cop at standing
up to the dark, richly flavoured and densely textured meat
of this most regal of birds. Most German white wines are
a little frail though for this purpose. As ever, Alsace
provides more fertile ground in the shape of its Pinot Gris,
Gewürztraminer and even Pinot Blanc wines. These varieties grown elsewhere should also suit the occasion. Red,
however, is a much more sensible idea, and anyway a
festive occasion without a good bottle of red seems a little
odd, to say the least. Big, burly Cabernets and Shirazes are
what's needed, whether from Australia (especially good),
California, South Africa or Chile. The biggest Rhône
wines, such as Hermitage, Cornas, Gigondas or the heavier
versions of Châteauneuf-du-Pape, are also impeccable
matches, as is a bottle of mature top-drawer claret. The
traditional potato stuffing, with sage and garlic, poses no
problems for red wine, but sharp, fruity relishes or a
fruitier stuffing, will. If you're going down the apple,
apricot or even prune route, one of those Alsace varietals
is definitely worth considering instead.

Grouse The most highly prized of the game birds, the
English season for which opens on 12 August, grouse
offers very flavourful dark meat that is best eaten after a
good period of hanging so that it achieves a high gaminess. In this state, it works well with mature red wines that
have their own gamey whiff about them, and also (if you
have the taste for them) with slightly sweet whites. In the
red corner, mature Pinot Noir is the surefire winner. Older
burgundy (i.e. with at least eight or so years in the bottle)
is a rare treat in this context if you can lay your hands on
one. Even among younger wines, it's Burgundian Pinot
that works best. Go with the likes of Gevrey-Chambertin,
Morey-St-Denis, Chambolle-Musigny, or any of the other
big Côte de Nuits names. A little gentler on the bank
balance is Fixin, a northerly appellation with a steadily

improving reputation. Some Chilean Pinots can work well with strong game, and even the odd Australian too. In the white corner, for sweetish whites, late-picked wines rather than those that have been botrytised (i.e. made from rotten grapes like Sauternes), are best. Look for the words 'Vendange Tardive' on Alsace wine labels of varietals such as Gewürztraminer, Pinot Gris or even Muscat, all of which are successful. Otherwise, try one of their non-European equivalents from California, Washington State or Australia.

Guinea-fowl The flesh of guinea-fowl isn't gamey at all, but is a densely textured white meat, a little like turkey in character but with superior flavour. It needs a rich and rounded dry white to do it justice, particularly if it is richly sauced, as it tends to be. Big, savoury wines that will oblige include Australian Semillon, Alsace Pinot Gris and Pinot Blanc, Rioja Crianza and other oaky Spanish whites from regions such as Navarra, and barrel-fermented Chardonnays from Chile, Australia or California, or (to extend the range) from Canada, Hungary or Sicily.

Ostrich Increasingly fashionable now, to the extent that the odd producer devoted to farming ostrich has cropped up in some decidedly chilly northern climes, the meat of the big bird is, as you would expect, dark and beefy, and fairly tough unless it has been tenderised or subjected to a long marination. It therefore needs the biggest reds, great strapping Syrah/Shiraz creations, including Australia's finest (with which it seems to have a particular affinity), as well as those from California, Chile, South Africa and the northern Rhône (where peppery Crozes-Hermitage and Hermitage itself are both good). Otherwise, Cabernet Sauvignon isn't a bad match, since ostrich will stand a fair amount of tannin in the wine. Bordeaux, Chile, California, even Austria provide fine examples.

Partridge Somewhat similar to guinea-fowl, in that it

provides a light, drily textured meat, but perhaps with a little more obvious gaminess in the flavour, partridge will rub along with much the same kinds of wines. Old burgundies and gently sweet whites are the order of the day. Aged Syrah from the Rhône or from Australia will also work. The grape, so ferocious in its youth, often seems to take on something of the gamey character of old Pinot Noir as it ages.

Pheasant Pheasant comes in a multitude of guises these days, depending on the age (and possibly the gender) of the bird, and how long it has been hung. It can be as bland as chicken, or almost as dark and high-tasting as grouse. Almost. It needs a slightly gentler wine than grouse, but along much the same sorts of lines. Pinot Noirs from California, Oregon, Spain or Burgundy are all great with pheasant (for Burgundy, go for one of the bigger wines of the Côte de Nuits, maybe Nuits St-Georges). Syrah, especially older Syrah, is fine too: choose Hermitage, Crozes-Hermitage or St-Joseph. Sweet, late-picked whites, though, are less good with pheasant for some reason. Best avoid.

Pigeon The meat of pigeon or squab is dark and rich, quite decadently so, but without the obvious gaminess of the true game birds. **Plainly roasted**, it needs a well-built red such as a Cabernet Sauvignon or Merlot from Chile, California, South Africa or Australia, or a blend based on those two grapes from the Médoc district of Bordeaux, Italian Nebbiolo thunderers like Barbaresco or Barolo, or one of the big-scale Spanish reds like Toro or Tarragona. **Baked in a pie**, as it often was during Second World War rationing in the UK, pigeon needs a slightly lighter red, but still one with a definite amount of heft. Australian Shiraz, southern Rhône reds like Gigondas, Lirac and Vacqueyras, or else a big Rioja Reserva, will all do the trick.

Quail A whole roast quail provides only enough meat to act as a rich but modestly proportioned starter dish. It's a dark meat and will be generally happier with a red wine, unless there is any sort of fruity stuffing (dried fruits were noticeably popular with quail a while back). With **plain-roasted** quail, midweight reds like Chianti Classico or other Sangiovese-based Italian reds, one of the lighter La Mancha or Valdepeñas reds from central Spain, a Ribatejo or Alentejo red blend from southern Portugal, or Merlots from Washington, California, Chile or the pays d'Oc will all do nicely. Another school of thought suggests that white wine is better with quail, but this is to overstate the delicacy of the meat. With one of those **fruity stuffings or sauces**, though, you might like to play safe with an acid-edged dry white such as Loire Sauvignon, South African Chenin, or Alsace or New Zealand Riesling.

Turkey The Christmas or Thanksgiving turkey is not, it has to be said, one of the gastronomic world's great riches, having the blandness of chicken, but with denser, tougher flesh. The breast meat can be extremely dry, but the darker meat of the legs offers more in the way of moistness, succulence and flavour. **Roasted** in the traditional way, it will take either a red or a white like chicken, but is probably happier – at a pinch – with a richly textured white. Certainly, anybody confining themselves to the **breast** should consider going down the opulent Chardonnay route: Burgundy, California, New Zealand, Chile, Argentina, Canada, central and eastern Europe and Australia are all brimming over with such wines. With the **dark meat** factored into the occasion, and perhaps a dollop of the traditional **sage and onion stuffing**, a mid-weight, soft-textured red will be a distinct possibility. Pinot Noir (Burgundy, Oregon, South Africa) and Merlot (Washington State, California, Australia, Chile) are all fine, and inexpensive Australian Shiraz works surprisingly well. Or you could try a strong Garnacha- or Syrah-based rosé from Spain or Argentina.

Woodcock Fairly similar to grouse, in that the meat is dark, strongly flavoured and gamey, but perhaps lacking that final dimension of intensity that grouse has, woodcock is a distinctly underrated game bird. What it requires is very definitely a red wine, but nothing too heavy: gentle tannins and middling weight are what to go for. Australian Cabernet-Shiraz blends, Merlots from California, Chile or South Africa, Portuguese Bairrada or Dão, Spain's Ribera del Duero, one of the gentler Nebbiolos of northwest Italy, or a Rhône red from either the north (St-Joseph, Cornas) or the south (Châteauneuf-du-Pape, Vacqueyras) of the region all make appetising matches. In a very old-school setting, it is traditional for woodcock to be served with the head split and a small spoon for scooping out the **brain**. This tiny, but pungently flavoured morsel requires the finest mature burgundy money can buy, although you will of course only need one mouthful of it.

7

MEAT (ANIMALS)

Having dealt with feathered meats in the preceding chapter, we now turn our attention to quadrupeds. These can be broadly divided into white and red meats, the former including pork, veal and rabbit, while the latter take in beef, lamb and venison, but we have listed one or two less obvious ones too. Once again, this simple division may have you harking back to the days of white wine with white meat and red wine with red. To hear the way some in the wine business go on, one would think that that basic rule, the pure and true logic of which saw our forebears' generations through a lifetime of untroubled dinners, was a piece of mystificatory hoodoo that could only hoodwink the unwary into getting things wrong.

In fact, it was a perfectly proper and readily understandable guideline. It is just that it is subject to rather more nuances, and the odd out-and-out exception, across the board, and these are worth bearing in mind. In any case, the great questions it left unanswered were: 'What type of white wine? What type of red?'

As with the poultry and game birds considered in Chapter 6, the choice of wine with these meats depends very much on their method of preparation, the degree of maturity and basic quality of the meat, and – crucially –

the seasoning and saucing to which they are treated. Vegetable or fruit accompaniments that are integral to the dish have some right to a say in the decision, but they should take a back seat. Only where some ingredient with a particularly pronounced flavour plays a central role in the complex of tastes in a dish – such as the red berries or juniper berries that are often served with venison, for example, or a downright obstreperous customer like globe artichoke – should it be taken into account when choosing the wine.

Otherwise, the key is not just to match the flavours of the wine to the seasoning and saucing, but to marry up the weight of the wine (measured in such factors as the extent – if any – of oak influence, its level of alcohol and its overall texture) to the texture of the meat. A tougher, or more fibrous, cut such as rump will require a bigger and burlier wine than will the gentler texture of a piece of fillet. The softer feel in the mouth generally imparted to a wine by new oak, where the producer has aged the wine in brand new, as opposed to used, barrels, is good with tender meats such as fillet steak or spring lamb, as is any wine that has distinct roundness of contour from low or age-softened acidity. Wines with spikier acidity, or young reds with pronounced tannin (the constituent of the grape-skins that contributes to that furry feeling in the mouth after drinking), are better with more sinewy meats, since they give the impression on the palate of helping to cut through the meat's texture.

Older vintages of fine wines should be reserved for particularly special occasions, and deserve to accompany the best meats. Butchers who are members of the Quality Guild mentioned in the last chapter will be able to supply these. Look out for rare-breed, organic meat that is hormone-free and hasn't been pumped with antibiotics, and always ask how long it has been hung for. Good beef such as Aberdeen Angus or Shorthorn, for instance, can take three to four weeks' hanging to ensure tenderness and flavour development. Simply and sensitively cooked, and not subjected to strong marinades or complicated sauces, the result of the care and attention lavished on it will be there on the plate for all to taste. And then your carefully chosen bottle will really come into its own.

BEEF

Beef bourguignonne This old bistro and dinner-party standby follows the same basic principle as coq au vin, in that it is cooked in a liquor of red wine (burgundy, specifically) with shallots, mushrooms, bacon and herbs, with chunks of stewing steak replacing the chicken, and the meat briefly flamed in cognac before the wine goes in. Somehow, it is never quite as satisfying a dish as coq au vin, perhaps because it lacks the slightly gelatinous consistency imparted by the chicken bones in the latter dish. And although it should be cooked in burgundy, it really needs a rather bigger, sturdier red to accompany it, because the meat in it is not of the tenderest cut. Languedoc reds, such as Corbières and Minervois, Cabernet Sauvignons from eastern Europe or South America, simple Australian Shiraz: these are all fine with it. If you want to stick to burgundy, though, go for one of the meatier ones – Mercurey, Pommard or Nuits St-Georges – but don't spend *too* much. This is basically a fairly rustic dish.

Beef sausages Although not everybody's first choice, sausages made purely of beef have their followers on dietary or religious grounds, and among those who fancy a change from the normal pork. They tend to be simultaneously thicker and looser in texture, even slightly shreddy, and need a correspondingly light-textured, but heartily fruity red to go with them. Merlot is a good grape variety choice. Buy varietal Merlots from Chile, California, Washington State or Bulgaria, or go for a Merlot-dominated blend with Cabernet, perhaps from the St-Emilion district of Bordeaux or from Australia. If they contain, as many do, a certain amount of strong spice such as **chilli, paprika and black pepper**, choose a simple Syrah like Crozes-Hermitage, or maybe one from California or Chile. With **Boston-style beef sausages**, which traditionally contain beer, it would seem odd to drink anything other than a lager-type light American beer.

Beef stew A cold-weather, English stew of braising steak with potatoes, carrots and onions, perhaps enriched in very un-English fashion with a good dollop of red wine, should be matched with a simple, robustly textured red with no airs and graces. Simple Cabernet Sauvignons from eastern and central Europe, Merlots from almost anywhere, inexpensive Shiraz from Australia or South Africa, or any of the southern French or northern Spanish blends based on Grenache (Garnacha) and Carignan (Cariñena) will do just fine, as would a traditional Portuguese red like Bairrada or Dão, or an inexpensive Nebbiolo from Italy's Piedmont region. As you can see, the palette is a broad one, and you can afford to be bold.

Beef Stroganoff The creamy, mushroomy stew that became popular in the 1960s is one of the few beef dishes that actually works better with white wine than with red, on account of the cream in the sauce. Richly flavoured whites, such as young white Rioja Crianza, barrel-fermented Chardonnays from California, Chile or Australia, Hunter Valley Semillons with a few years' bottle-age, or dry white Bordeaux will do the trick. The other grape that works very well with Stroganoff is Riesling, which is often a good bet with a creamy sauce. Australia and New Zealand are the best places to look.

Beef Wellington A very regal dish of beef fillet baked in a golden coat of puff pastry, beef Wellington deserves a rather opulent wine. Our first choice would be a good claret, but one of the gentler wines of St-Emilion or Pomerol, rather than the harder, more tannic-edged examples from the Médoc. Even these Merlot-dominated wines, though, retain a certain degree of acerbity, which marries well with the butteriness of the pastry. Ripe, rounded Cabernet Sauvignons from Argentina and Chile, Chianti Classico from a fine vintage, and Ribera del Duero from northern Spain are good matches, and so are the more muscular wines of Beaujolais (i.e. Moulin-à-Vent, Morgon, Côte de Brouilly). There are those who claim that the relative plainness of flavour in the dish is such that the right white wine can just about cope with it. If you feel like bucking the trend, go for an Alsace Pinot Gris or perhaps a high-alcohol South African Colombard for their weight.

Burgers You won't of course find a wine list in McDonalds, but say you have rustled up some home-made burgers using best-quality ground beef, or say you have just been out to the kind of takeaway where they cook the burgers to order in front of you on a flame grill, and you now want to drink a nice glass of wine with your meal. Almost any simple red, provided it isn't too piercingly fruity, will complete the scene. Ordinary Côtes du Rhône or Côtes du Rhône-Villages, or Côtes du Roussillon, Fitou, Vacqueyras or pays d'Oc Cabernet-Merlot blends are the French options. Otherwise, an everyday Australian Shiraz, Washington State or Chilean Merlot (but not of Reserve quality) or South African Pinotage will all suit too. **Cheeseburgers** can take a fruitier wine. Cabernets from Chile, Australia or California perform well here, and so does the peppery edge of northern Rhône Syrah, e.g. Crozes-Hermitage.

Chilli con carne Everybody has their own favourite

formula for this popular Mexican dish of minced beef, red beans and peppers, all fired up with generous quantities of whole chillies or chilli powder. The other essential spice in the dish is ground cumin, a little of which goes a long way, and which to some extent skews the match with wine more than that red-hot chilli does. Big and spicy is what the dish is looking for in its wine partner, so think Syrah/Shiraz, Nebbiolo or Zinfandel. An Australian Shiraz or Shiraz-Cabernet blend is a delight with chilli, as is a robustly textured Châteauneuf-du-Pape or Gigondas from the southern Rhône. The lighter versions of muscled-up Barolo and Barbaresco from Piedmont in northwest Italy work well, and so – even more so, in fact – does Californian Zinfandel. Nailing your colours to the Tex-Mex mast, you might set out for a Texan red and, failing to find one in your local wine merchant, as is quite likely, opt instead for a Mexican Cabernet Sauvignon or Petite Sirah. The latter grape (nothing to do with Syrah itself) is something of a speciality in Mexico. It produces a damsony, peppery red more than capable of giving chilli con carne a run for its money.

Corned beef hash The pronounced saltiness of this traditional English dish mean that it will accept a wine with a perceptible degree of residual sweetness to it. That could mean Zinfandel from California or Chile, or a Californian or Australian Pinot Noir. What it actually prefers, though, on the quiet, is a white wine. Gewürztraminer and Pinot Gris from Alsace, the United States or New Zealand all fit the bill of fare, as does German Riesling with a touch of sugar-ripeness (look for Kabinett or Spätlese on the label).

Cottage pie A thoroughly homely dish of minced beef with onions and carrots baked under a mashed potato top, English cottage pie will rub along contentedly with an everyday red that has no harsh edges. Those southern Rhône blends are unfailingly useful again (from simple

Côtes du Rhône up to Lirac or Vacqueyras), or drink a Spanish Rioja Crianza, or Valpolicella Classico from northeast Italy. South African and Chilean Merlots are fine, and a Shiraz-Cabernet blend from South Australia would also do nicely.

Goulash The gentle spiciness in this traditional Hungarian stewed dish comes from paprika, which is added in far more generous quantities on its home turf than cooks in other countries dare get away with. A Hungarian red would be an ethnically unimpeachable match. (Remember the old Bull's Blood? Now forget it, and pick up one of Hungary's more modern offerings, made from Cabernet Sauvignon or Merlot or both.) Failing that, any other eastern European Cabernet or Merlot will oblige, or go for a Shiraz-Cabernet blend from Australia. A touch of spice in the wine won't go at all amiss. Australian Grenache, one of northern Portugal's modern Douro reds, or even Mexico's Petite Sirah will all work. Mexican wine with a Hungarian dish? This must be what we mean by being adventurous.

Lasagne/Spaghetti Bolognese The meat sauce with these two dishes is essentially the same thing – a herby, oniony mélange of minced beef and tomato. Lasagne adds the complicating factor of a creamy béchamel sauce, though. **Spag bol** first: like lasagne, the dish is naturally crying out for an Italian wine. Tuscany is the happiest hunting-ground, with Chianti Classico, Brunello and Rosso di Montalcino, and Carmignano all passing muster. Southern Italy should not be overlooked, though. Aglianico del Vulture from Basilicata in the southwest makes a fine match too. Italian varietals from elsewhere (California, Argentina and Australia) also play their parts well. With **lasagne**, something a little less sharp than those Sangiovese-based Tuscans seems best. Montepulciano d'Abruzzo from the Adriatic coast is a winner, as is the lighter style of Cabernet produced in the northerly Trentino region, and Piedmont's Dolcetto and Barbera varietals. Merlots from the Veneto, in the northeast, can be good, but may prove a little too light in some cases. Otherwise, look to those Bonardas from Argentina.

Meatloaf A beef-based meatloaf, perhaps bulked with pork as well, can take a slightly more upmarket wine than you might expect. Its relatively simple, oniony flavour works well with soft-textured reds made from the Pinot Noir and Gamay grape varieties. For the former, choose a California, Oregon or New Zealand wine, with good burgundy as a back-up choice (Beaune or Pommard, say). Gamay, the Beaujolais grape, is perhaps even better. A cru wine with two or three years' bottle-age will be sublime. Fleurie, Chiroubles or Chénas would be our tips. If you come across it, Californian Gamay is a good substitute.

Oxtail This particularly robust cut of beef is usually rendered glutinous in texture from long cooking, but the meat itself should be impeccably tender and fall away from the bone with ease. A rich, but not too tannic red is best. Earthy Californian Merlots, Chilean Cabernet Sauvignons, Châteauneuf-du-Pape, Pomerol from Bordeaux, and Australian Cabernets or Cabernet-Shiraz blends are the kinds of wines to consider.

Roast beef Depending on the particular cut, traditional plainly roasted beef will take a midweight to heavyish red, but nothing too monstrous. Old-fashioned Barolo or Hermitage will quite likely overwhelm it. Rare-roasted topside even makes a sympathetic partner to a surprisingly light red, such as one from the Loire (Chinon or Saumur-Champigny). A particularly fond memory is of a Morgon from Beaujolais that went beautifully with a piece of lightly roasted beef fillet. Otherwise, look to the Rhône and Bordeaux in France, the medium-bodied reds of Spain or Portugal (the latter, from the Alentejo for example, are notably good with roast beef), or the Cabernet-Shiraz or Cabernet-Merlot blends of Australia, California or Chile. With **cold roast beef**, a ripe rosé can be sublime, especially if the meat has a blush of pink in the centre. A Bordeaux, Hungarian or Chilean Cabernet-based rosé works like a dream. If you are partial to **horseradish sauce** with beef, then up the ante with the wine, and choose something stronger and spicier (see the guidelines under **Chilli con carne** for inspiration).

Steak A grilled, fried or barbecued steak is a very forgiving dish for wine. Provided you stick to red, there's no need to tiptoe around it, even if it's an expensive piece of prime fillet. The rarer you like your steak, the softer in texture you might wish the wine to be. A **chargrilled** steak, with the singed aroma of the mesquite grill on it in the southern States fashion, will probably want a reasonably big Californian customer – a Syrah, say, or a Cabernet Sauvignon. Then again, a mature Beaujolais, such as Moulin-à-Vent or Morgon, makes an almost equally obliging partner. With a **creamy mustard or peppercorn sauce**, go for spice and acidity in the wine. Italian Barbera, Tuscan reds, Spanish Tempranillo-based blends and even well-built Pinot Noir (Californian or New Zealand) work well. The high-intensity hotness of **steak au poivre**, or classic **black pepper sauce**, need a strong, perhaps slightly sweetish red to cope with them. Californian Zinfandel, South African Pinotage, Australian Shiraz and Rioja Reserva are all suitably hot favourites.

Steak and kidney pie A warming supper dish from another era, a good steak-and-kidney pie or pudding has a comforting quality to it all its own. It needs a softish, but strongly flavoured wine to match the gamey pungency of the kidneys. Mature wines (say, at least five years old) cope well, either made from Pinot Noir (including burgundy), or from Spain's Tempranillo grape

(Rioja or Navarra). Gently textured Cabernets are fine too – an eastern European or Italian example will do nicely – and the undemanding nature of many inexpensive Argentinian reds seems just right.

Steak tartare A perplexing dish if ever there was one, since it contains both raw beef and raw egg, steak tartare nonetheless has its devotees, and is even still to be found on the occasional restaurant menu. It has an aggressive spicy edge too, from the use of Worcestershire sauce, and remains quite hard to partner with wine. Oddly enough, light fruity Italian reds fare reasonably well: Dolcetto, Valpolicella, even featherlight Bardolino. Then again, and taking lightness to its logical conclusion, a white wine tends to be a more apposite match than a red. Simple unoaked Chardonnay with pronounced acidity is a safe enough course, as are Italian whites such as Soave.

HAM/GAMMON

These salty pork cuts are best with relatively light wines that won't overwhelm the flavour of the meat, although the preparations as always should have a say in the matter. With a **baked or roast ham**, studded with cloves and as often as not given a honey-based glaze, a light red with pronounced fruitiness is best. Beaujolais's Gamay grape is lovely with ham, and running it close are Cabernet Franc and Pinot Noir. The red wines of the Loire, such as Chinon, Saumur-Champigny or Bourgueil, are varietal Cabernet Franc, and good choices if the vintage is a ripe and juicy one, or try one of the lighter burgundies (Savigny-lès-Beaune, Givry or Hautes-Côtes-de-Beaune) or their non-European counterparts (New Zealand or Oregon). **Cold roast ham**, or boiled ham, with salad is better off with a light off-dry white, perhaps a Mosel Riesling of Kabinett or Spätlese quality, or a medium-dry Chenin Blanc. Better still, though, is a rosé, which seems

just made for cold ham. Southern France or northern
Spain, where the blends are of pretty much the same
grapes, are the tops. For a **grilled gammon steak**, go with
either the rosé or light red theme, with a cru Beaujolais
(Fleurie, Juliénas) or California Gamay topping the bill
among the latter.

HARE

The amazingly rich and flavourful meat of hare is too
little used. Nothing like rabbit, it's dark and strong –
exactly what game should be. The old English dish of
jugged hare, or indeed any **stew** that contains both blood
and wine, such as a French *civet*, needs a mature but
robust red wine to accompany it. Nebbiolos from northwest Italy (Barbaresco and Barolo) would do it justice, as
would a mature (i.e. at least five-year-old) top northern
Rhône, such as Hermitage or Côte-Rôtie. Burgundy, the
traditional game partner, tends to be a bit too delicate for
it, but a more muscular Pinot Noir from California,
Australia or Chile would work. Another fashionable
French method of preparing hare is to serve it **braised
with green grapes**, which needs a slightly lighter, fruitier
wine, but still a red one. One of the bigger Beaujolais
(Morgon or Moulin-à-Vent) would be great, but a midweight Italian red, such as Montepulciano d'Abruzzo, is
fine too. The bright, strawberryish flavours of Oregon
Pinot Noir would suit it to a tee.

KANGAROO

First appearing on northern-hemisphere restaurant menus
in the early 1990s, the meat of kangaroo is, not surprisingly, fairly tough, sinewy and dry. It needs tenderising
and/or marinating, but when well-seasoned (they add
plenty of assertive spice to it in Pacific Rim cooking), it
has the chunky appeal of richly flavoured beefsteak. You

won't expect us to look much further afield than its native country for a suitable wine match, and indeed it is hard to imagine any better partner for it than premium Australian Shiraz. That said, a Shiraz blend with Cabernet Sauvignon is fine too, and so is South Australian Merlot. If you want to be awkward, go to South Africa or Chile for your next best choices, sticking with those same grape varieties. Determined Francophiles will be relieved to hear they can drink a nice, mature Médoc claret with it without doing any damage to the wine.

KID

The roasted meat of the young male goat is a traditional peasant dish in parts of Spain and Greece. Despite its rather strong aroma, it isn't a particularly flavourful meat, having something of the lightness of flavour of young spring lamb. As such, it tends to have bundles of herbs thrown at it before cooking, which give it a savoury pungency it would otherwise lack. Reserva-class Spanish reds, such as Rioja, Navarra or Valdepeñas, have the requisite softness of texture. If in Greece, do as the locals do, and drink Nemea, Naoussa, Liatiko or Goumenissa reds with it. Simple burgundies will come to no harm either.

LAMB

Grilled lamb steaks, etc. Cutlets, leg steaks or chops done under the grill are good with the same kinds of wines as are suited to roast lamb, but you may not want to push the boat out quite as much. Simple Cabernet-Merlot blends from just about anywhere, or hearty Spanish or Portuguese reds, will not let the side down.

Irish stew Stewed with plenty of chunky potatoes and carrots, lamb makes a spirits-lifting winter supper dish. Choose an equally hearty, but not too assertively fruit-laden, red to go with it. A southern Italian wine, such as

Aglianico del Vulture, Salice Salentino or a Negroamaro-Cabernet blend, would make a refreshing change. Spanish Tempranillo-based blends are good, as are any of the older Portuguese appellations, like Dão and Bairrada. South Africa's Pinotage, never the most food-friendly of grapes, behaves itself in this company, and straightforward, not-too-expensive Australian Shiraz works as well.

Kleftiko This favourite of the old-school Greek tavernas, lamb on the bone cooked long and slow until it attains an almost miraculous degree of tempting tenderness, is a very appealing dish. Start with Greek reds, if your local wine merchant has any. Xynomavro is a fine red grape variety, which goes into the wines of Naoussa. Cyprus wines lag considerably behind those of Greece in quality, but Lebanon has some brilliant, sturdy reds comparable to the bigger vintages of Bordeaux. The dish is nothing without fistfuls of fresh herbs, principally thyme, and a savoury edge in the wine is needed to match them. If you can't therefore lay your hands on any eastern Mediterranean reds, a middle-ranking claret from St-Julien or Pauillac will be equally fitting. In the southern hemisphere, South Africa, Chile and Argentina are probably best for Cabernets, Merlots or blends thereof.

Lancashire hotpot Chunks of lamb slow-cooked with potatoes, carrots, turnip or swede, and usually served with slices of beetroot, this dish can be eaten with much the same wines as are appropriate with Irish stew. The flavours are just a little more assertive, though, and pickled beetroot will hammer the subtleties out of a classy red. Keep it simple, then, and add some of the lighter, northern wines to that list of Italians suggested under Irish stew. Barbera or Dolcetto from Piedmont, and Teroldego from Trento would all be good, as would Squinzano, another southern star from Puglia. Australia's Mataro, usually blended with

Shiraz, makes a good match with the vegetables in the dish, or try your luck with a Grenache or Grenache-based blend from South Australia.

Moussaka Another one for those Greek reds, if you can find them, the baked dish of minced lamb with aubergine, béchamel sauce and (very often, but not quite correctly) potato too, was most people's introduction to Greek cooking. Naoussa from northern Greece is a good bet. Some North African reds, from the likes of Morocco or Tunisia, are fine. They don't necessarily have a great deal of stuffing, but the fact that the lamb in the dish is minced means it can take a lighter wine. Otherwise, Spanish reds from some of the lesser-known regions, such as Somontano or Calatayud, are worth trying, as are Portuguese reds from the Ribatejo or Alentejo regions, or inexpensive, rustic Pinot Noirs from eastern Europe, Chile or South Africa.

Mutton There is hardly any call at all now for the meat of older sheep, and most butchers will probably look askance at you if you ask for it. It is inevitably tougher, and can suffer from a peculiar waxy flavour derived from the wool fat. Mutton widely gave way in the early years of the twentieth century to the more tender meat of the younger animal. Once in a blue moon, however, particularly in southern Europe, it is possible still to come across it. Eat it with one of the sturdiest reds of whichever country you happen to be in: Spain, Portugal, Italy, Greece. If in France, drink an old Rhône red with it (Châteauneuf-du-Pape or Gigondas). Australian Shiraz would also make a good match.

Roast lamb There are ultimately only two really incomparable matches with roast lamb, one of which is a fine, mature claret and the other Rioja Reserva. It follows, though, that other Tempranillo-based Spanish blends, and blends of Cabernet Sauvignon and Merlot, shouldn't be far behind them, and indeed they aren't. Very ripe, blackcurrant fruit can slightly get in the way if the lamb has been seasoned with **rosemary** but otherwise left quite plain (stick with Bordeaux in that case), but does come into its own if there is anything fruity in the gravy, such as **redcurrants**. Choices might then be made from Australian, Californian or Chilean Cabernet Sauvignon. If a pungent glaze of **garlic, mustard, lemon and herbs** is applied, those Spanish reds will taste like heaven, but strong, slightly tannic Pinot Noir – as in California, Chile or even New Zealand – will work almost as successfully. If you like old-fashioned vinegary **mint sauce** with your lamb, ratchet down the wine quality by several notches. It is very hard indeed on the flavours of wine, and a really good bottle will, quite honestly, be wasted on it.

Shepherd's pie Much the same as a cottage pie, only made with minced lamb instead of minced beef, this warming mash-topped supper dish needs an everyday red with reasonably soft texture. Blends of Syrah, Grenache, etc. from the Languedoc and Roussillon regions of southern France show up well (think St-Chinian, Minervois, Faugères). Barbera or Sangiovese reds from Italy, Portuguese Douro Valley blends, and any of the Cabernet/Merlot permutations of eastern Europe are all fine, and Australian blends containing Grenache seem to be a good idea.

PORK

Casseroled pork A light-textured stew of cubed pork with tomatoes, peppers, onions and white wine will, like many another such recipe, take a white or a light red wine, according to taste. Whites should be quite strong in alcohol to reflect the fact that it's a meat dish, but not too overtly fruity. Pinot Blanc from Alsace, white Rioja or Macabeo-Chardonnay blends from Spain, South African Chenin Blanc or Colombard, or unoaked (or very lightly oaked) Australian Chardonnay are all appropriate. Reds should tack to the gentler side, with minimal tannin and not too much alcohol (i.e. not more than 13%). That means Languedoc and Loire reds, La Mancha and Valdepeñas from Spain, or Pinot Noirs from Chile or South Africa.

Pork chops Plain grilled pork chops are happiest with a lightish red equipped with a fair amount of acidity to cut through the fattiness. Young Pinot Noir fits the bill (Burgundy's Mercurey or Côte de Beaune-Villages will do quite well), as does the tart, light style of Beaujolais (Brouilly, Juliénas, Chénas or Beaujolais-Villages), Californian Gamay, or Italy's Dolcetto.

Pork in mustard sauce A bistro favourite in which a soft-textured piece of pork (e.g. tenderloin) is served in a reduction sauce combining white wine or fino sherry, Dijon or wholegrain mustard (or both) and cream, this dish emphatically needs a rich white wine. Like all cream sauces, it's probably happiest with a richly buttery, creamy Chardonnay, but the sharpness of the mustard calls for some noticeable acidity too. Cooler-climate wines from the likes of Chile's Casablanca Valley, Tasmania or one of the coastal regions of South Africa will work very well, as would a good, ripe Chablis. Alsace comes up trumps again, with both Pinot Gris and Riesling showing well.

Pork Normandy style Another creamy-sauced pork dish, this one is made of cider or calvados (or both), with sliced apples and cream. A fruitier note in the accompanying white will help matters here, to match the apple. A barrel-aged Sauvignon Blanc, from Chile or New Zealand, is a good bet, as are Australian Marsanne or Verdelho, or an oaky dry white Bordeaux from the Pessac-Léognan district. There are no wines made in Normandy, but there is of course a lot of cider, and one of the quality medium-dry ones (in a bottle with a champagne-style cork) would be the obvious choice with this dish. Still thinking fizz, a richly textured blanc de noirs champagne might just stay the distance too.

Pork pie A good-quality English pork pie, with a rich pastry crust, savoury jelly, and fine pale brown meat that hasn't been treated with saltpetre, is one of the great picnic foods. All it needs to go with it is a generous heap of lightly dressed green salad, and some unflavoured salted crisps (potato chips). The wine it would like is white and dry, with gentle green fruit, and enough crisply citric acidity to cut through the density of the pastry. Loire Sauvignon (Sancerre, Pouilly-Fumé, Menetou-Salon) is a banker with pork pie, having all these attributes in just the right balance. Vouvray sec isn't bad, and one of the fruitier versions of Muscadet (yes, there are one or two out there) is good too. From outside Europe, dry Riesling is a pretty sympathetic match: go to Australia's Clare Valley, New Zealand or California for the right mix of flavours.

Pork sausages There are so many different variations on the basic pork sausage formula now that it would be impossible to exhaust them, and all their possible wine combinations, here. As a very general rule, sausages are happier with a light to midweight red wine with a cutting-edge of acidity to counteract any fattiness. For **Cumberland sausages**, Italian reds are great (Chianti, Barbera, Dolcetto, even Veneto Merlot all work well), and so are Portugal's Alentejo reds. Simple Côtes du Rhône (or Côtes du Roussillon) makes sense too, as do blends of Grenache and Syrah from around the world. **Lincolnshire sausages**, with their strong note of dried sage, need a rather sharper red. Those Italian wines will all do, but better still would be a youthful Beaujolais, such as Fleurie. With a garlicky, **Toulouse-style sausage**, more pungency of flavour in the wine is called for. Older Pinot Noir and Spanish Reserva reds are good, or perhaps a South African Cabernet with three or four years' bottle-age. A spicy sausage made with **chilli,**

paprika and black pepper needs a spicy wine, so reach for the peppery, northern Rhône Syrah reds (Crozes-Hermitage, St-Joseph). Spanish **chorizo** needs the biggest, spiciest red of all. Spain's own Toro or Tarragona are brilliant, but those Rhône reds, or Australian or Californian Shiraz/Syrah, are also great, as is California's Zinfandel and southern Italy's Primitivo. If the sausage contains pieces of fruit, such as **orange or apricot**, you might just get away with a white wine, but make it a big one, such as a Gewürztraminer from Chile, New Zealand or Alsace, or an Austrian Grüner Veltliner. With **frankfurters**, the only unimpeachable match is of course with German wine, but don't head straight for the Riesling. The gentler flavours of Weissburgunder (Pinot Blanc), Grauburgunder or Ruländer (Pinot Gris) or Silvaner (as in Frankenwein) are much better, even with **smoked frankfurters**.

Roast pork Plain-roasted pork, with its crackling all crisped up to perfection, is a very easy-going dish when it comes to wine. The roasty flavours, enhanced by crunchy roast potatoes, might seem to prefer a red wine, but richly textured whites, balanced by a hint of lemony acidity, will work just as well. Reds should be Pinot Noir, Gamay, Grenache, Sangiovese or Tempranillo, or blends based thereon, while whites can run the gamut from Chardonnay through Pinot Gris to Riesling. A slightly sweet German Rheingau or Pfalz Riesling (Kabinett or Spätlese), or a Vendange Tardive Riesling from Alsace, or a late-picked version from California or Washington State, are all wonderful with the traditional **apple sauce** accompaniment to roast pork.

RABBIT

The meat of rabbit is mostly very light and delicately flavoured, often quite astoundingly similar to chicken, and it will therefore take much the same wines as chicken, with a slight bias towards the red end of the spectrum. Cooked in the classic way with **mustard**, it is best with a sharply contoured Italian red such as Valpolicella, young Chianti or Rosso di Montalcino, but other interesting matches would be Californian Gamay, Fleurie from Beaujolais, Australia's Tarrango, or one of the gentler versions of South African Pinotage. A fashionable restaurant dish of recent times has been rabbit **stuffed with black pudding**, which needs a fairly heavy-duty red. Gigondas, Australian Shiraz or Washington State Merlot are all good matches. If the rabbit is cubed up and cooked in a **light casserole**, you can serve a light red or sturdy rosé with it. Rosados from Spain or Argentina, or Tavel from the Rhône, will oblige.

VEAL

Depending on the method of cooking, veal tends to be a very lightly flavoured meat. Thin-cut escalopes are a mainstay of old-school Italian trattorias (where they call them scallopini), and come variously sauced. With a **creamy mustard sauce**, the same wines can be drunk as are suggested above for pork in mustard sauce. With a darker, richer, sweeter **marsala sauce**, the wine match becomes trickier. A light red seems better than a white, but choose one with good, ripe fruit. Valpolicella Classico should do the trick. **Saltimbocca**, in which the veal is wrapped up in ham with herbs and braised in white wine, is better with an Italian white such as Vernaccia di San Gimignano or Verdicchio, or at a pinch a light rosé, but choose one from the south of France or northern Spain, rather than one of the generally vapid Italian specimens. **Wiener schnitzel**, or **cotoletta alla Milanese** (breaded, fried escalopes, depending on whether you're in Austria or Italy), bring us right back to white wine territory. Dry German Rieslings (labelled Trocken), Grüner Veltliner and other white varietals from Austria, and northern Italian whites such as Gavi, Bianco di Custoza, Soave Classico or Pinot Grigio, will all make discreet partners for what is in effect rather a bland dish, as would a Pinot Gris from Oregon or one from Canada. With **osso bucco**, the Italian dish of veal knuckle stewed with tomatoes, onions, citrus zests and white wine, a heartier red is called for: Brunello di Montalcino, one of the lighter Nebbiolos of Piedmont (i.e. not Barolo or Barbaresco), a Ribera del Duero from Spain, or an Alentejo blend from Portugal.

VENISON

The meat of deer, although technically classified as game, isn't as richly or gamily flavoured as first-timers might expect. It's not a million miles away from the flavour of good, sinewy beef, but with less fat resulting in a faintly drier texture. A **roast haunch of venison** is the kind of dish that has people harking back to the days of Tudor banquets, but the thin German wines they drank with it then most certainly won't do. It needs big, burly creations, such as Hermitage from the Rhône, Italy's Barolo, Spain's Toro or Ribera del Duero reds, a big Ribatejo number from Portugal, or Cabernet Sauvignon from California or Argentina. With **red berries** in the sauce, Merlot will prove slightly more fitting, whether from Washington State, California or Chile, and with the currently fashionable accompaniment of **juniper berries**, it will benefit from the gentle astringency of Italian reds such as Tuscany's Rosso di Montalcino, Puglia's Squinzano or one of the Sicilian blends. Much the same wines as for roast venison will also go with **plain-grilled venison steaks**. If the meat is **stewed or casseroled**, go for something a little less opulent. Medium-quality clarets, southern Rhône blends such as Vacqueyras, Italian blends of Negroamaro and Cabernet Sauvignon from Puglia, and Shiraz-Grenache blends from Australia are all suitable.

8

OFFAL

There is nothing like the demand for these miscellaneous types of meat these days, largely because, as the twentieth century wore on, people became more squeamish about eating anything that looked too much like part of an animal. This is to be regretted, not only because the internal organs are often the richest and tastiest items to be had (compare the flavour of a meltingly tender piece of calf's liver to that of a slab of fillet steak, for example), but also because they are more nutritious, and considerably lower in fat, than the prime cuts. A certain amount is used in processed foods such as pies and pâtés, but as the centrepiece of a main course, they are definitely falling from favour. We see many restaurant menus today that offer none of the meats listed in this chapter among their main-course options.

The problem might be somewhat ameliorated if we found another English word to refer to them, 'offal' having unfortunate connotations nowadays of the waste products left over after the choicer cuts have been accounted for. Among hunting and gathering communities in the past, exactly the opposite was considered to be the case. The men whose job it was to track down and kill an animal would customarily make themselves an instant meal of the internal organs on the spot, partly because they degrade more quickly than the muscle tissue, but also because they were considered to be the best parts. In the United States, the organs are known as 'variety meats', a meaningless enough phrase in itself, but one whose use probably keeps sales of them more buoyant than they would otherwise be.

Furthermore, this is a bountiful hunting ground for wine-matching, as the rich and assertive flavours of these meats generally call for big, forthright, even rather grand wines. If the last time you bought a piece of liver, or ordered it in a restaurant, is lost to living memory, now is the time to try it again. And if you hadn't previously thought of drinking wine with it, you are in for an extremely pleasant surprise.

Brains While there are very few people willing to prepare these at home nowadays, they have been sighted on the odd restaurant menu at places that specialise in contemporary cooking that tries to expand customers' horizons. A renowned French chef in London has successfully served a first course of lightly battered brain fritters with a sharply flavoured herbed mayonnaise, the dish having been well enough received to have sold out by halfway through the evening. Brains have an intensely rich, savoury flavour that is best matched with a well-built, dry white wine lacking nothing in punch. Mature *premier cru* Chablis makes a superb match, with the slight pungency the wine takes on after three or four years in the bottle serving the purpose admirably. A lightly oaked Chardonnay from just about anywhere else would also do (California probably the best option), but too much oak could well amount to an embarrassment of richness. Viognier with a little bottle-age (say, a couple of years on from the vintage) works too, when its initial burst of lemon tang has had chance to subside, and the gentler, mildly spicy, apricotty flavours have come through. Try one from California or the south of France (best of all from Condrieu in the northern Rhône).

Kidneys Densely textured **calf's kidneys** should be cooked very gently, so as to avoid toughness. With a meat stock sauce and mashed potato, they make a fitting dish for the most capacious appetite. Best wines with them are big, soft-hearted reds, such as Cabernet Sauvignon or Merlot, or blends of the two, from Chile, California, Washington State, Australia or the Médoc district of Bordeaux, but try not to go for wines of less than five years old from Bordeaux, or less than three from outside Europe. With **lamb's kidneys**, which are obviously smaller and more tender, a softer red is better. Pinot Noir is a good match, either from the United States (California or Oregon), or from one of the gentler appellations of Burgundy (Beaune, perhaps). A cru Beaujolais such as Fleurie or St-Amour works well, as does the gently oaky style of Rioja Crianza. For steak and kidney pie, see the beef section of Chapter 7.

Liver The best liver of all is **calf's liver**, which has the tenderest texture and the smoothest flavour. Quickly grilled so as to leave a trace of pink in the centre, it is one of the grandest dishes in this chapter. What it wants is a gentle, reasonably mature red with subtle, underlying power. Some of Italy's reds fit this bill perfectly. Nebbiolo from Piedmont can be a great match, but not if it's made in the old-fashioned super-tannic style of much Barolo. Wines like Nebbiolo delle Langhe, or the Nebbiolo-based Gattinara, are considerably easier on both purse and palate. A fine, single-vineyard Valpolicella Classico (not the basic village wine) has the right degree of stuffing, as does Montepulciano d'Abruzzo, although its flavours are not quite as complex. Châteauneuf-du-Pape is a very sympathetic match, now that it tends to be made in a

lighter style than of old, and other southern Rhône reds
such as Lirac or Vacqueyras, or Languedoc wines like
St-Chinian or Costières de Nîmes, are likewise successful.
Outside Europe, best bets are Syrah-Grenache blends
from Australia or California, or even California's
Zinfandel for its roundness, its mellow spice and its long
finish. **Lamb's liver and pig's liver** can be tougher and less
distinguished in flavour, and need a correspondingly less
exalted wine to go with them. Something like ordinary
Côtes du Rhône-Villages, Gamay de Touraine, eastern
European Merlot or Cabernet Sauvignon, or South
Africa's Pinotage are fine. Cooking liver with **bacon and
onions** in the traditional way helps the matching with
wine no end, and will open up new possibilities along the
above lines.

Sweetbreads Calf's and lamb's sweetbreads (which are
the thalamus and not, as is often supposed, anything to do
with testicles) are not as rich as many other organ meats,
but do have a deservedly high standing among gastro-
nomes, on account of their gently creamy texture. For that
very attribute, they need a gently creamy white wine to
accompany them. Reds simply taste too metallic with
sweetbreads. Soave Classico can make an unexpectedly
constructive match, as can Colombard or Colombard-
Chardonnay blends from South Africa, blends
of Chardonnay and Macabeo from Spain, and blends of
Semillon and Chardonnay from Australia. Viognier isn't
bad, although if very young, it can be a little too piercingly
fruity, while the sturdily built, unoaked whites of the
Rhône, such as the white versions of Châteauneuf-du-
Pape or St-Joseph, or even white Côtes du Rhône-Villages,
offer good textural counterpoint. As always, there are
good matches to be found in Alsace, particularly the more
opulent versions of Pinot Blanc or Sylvaner. **Rich sauces**
will allow you to up the richness quotient in the wine, with

lightly oaked Chardonnays and white Riojas coming into their own with anything creamy.

Tongue Served as a **cooked dish**, for a main course, tongue needs a gentle red wine, such as a Gamay from Beaujolais, Touraine or California, Italian Dolcetto, Austrian Blaufränkisch, or even one of Germany's rare reds from the Dornfelder grape. A more mainstream choice might be a Reserve-quality Merlot from eastern Europe or Chile. Presented **cold**, as often as not as a first course, a white wine is better. High-acid, fruity wines are right, so head towards Sauvignon or Chenin Blanc territory, with wines from the Loire, South Africa or New Zealand all outstanding.

Tripe Once a popular choice from fish and chip shops in the north of England, tripe has also largely disappeared from the dinner table. Served steaming-hot **with onions**, all it needs is a simple, fairly acid-edged white wine of no great distinction. Well-chilled Muscadet, dry Vouvray, or one of the dry whites of northern Italy, such as Soave, Albana di Romagna or Bianco di Custoza, will all do. Its best hope of staging a return to favour is to serve it in the Spanish fashion, in a **tomatoey stew** containing onions, peppers and perhaps the odd chunk of chorizo to help it along. In this form, it clearly needs a richly flavoured, midweight red. Spain's own examples of these from Rioja, Navarra, Calatayud or El Bierzo are all wonderful with this dish, or try a Portuguese red from the Alentejo, a Grenache or Tarrango from Australia, or an Argentinian Malbec.

9

ETHNIC AND VEGETARIAN CUISINES

The days when a guide such as this would have completed its work once it had told you what to eat with grilled trout and roast beef, with perhaps a little suet pudding to follow, are (happily enough) long gone. We now have, in the Western world, an unprecedented – and seemingly ever-expanding – range of the world's cuisines to choose from. Indeed, nobody is in the least surprised any longer to find representative dishes of different cuisines sitting side by side with each other on the same restaurant menu. Much of this cheerful diversity is to be celebrated. Some aspects of it are not so uplifting. We don't, for example, have to have everything on the same plate, adding Thai spicing to a Japanese-style sushi roll made with turmeric-scented Indian rice. And a Peking Duck pizza is a crime that cries to heaven for vengeance.

Notwithstanding the outbreak of the magpie approach to the world's culinary cultures, there is much to be celebrated in this fertile cross-pollination. The palette of flavours that the wholesale discovery of east Asian cookery in particular has made possible to Western cooks has been a force for liberation, bringing seasonings such as garlic, ginger and chilli into the mainstream culinary repertoire for the first time. We are (just) of an age to recall a time in the UK when the sight of fresh ginger root in the produce section of the supermarket was a cause for some wonderment. Nowadays, one clicks one's tongue (or worse) to find that they're fresh out. This is all to the good, but what implications does it have for wine?

The short answer is that it opens up whole new possibilities, and the longer version is this chapter. For many years, there was an assumption – bolstered by the nervous advice given by certain food and wine commentators of the old school – that most of the dishes referred to here were simply not fit partners for wine. At least, if you positively insisted on drinking wine with them, you were far better off sticking to something very basic, almost invariably white, and chilled to within an inch of its life. The logic was that the ferocious spicing in Indian cooking, and the often sticky-sweet sauces in Chinese, were no friends to decent wine. They denuded such wine of its subtleties, and left you having spent an uncomfortable amount of money on something that you couldn't now taste. To some extent, this was justified by the rather crude artist's impressions of Indian and Chinese food that we were at first introduced to in the West, but now that we know our bhajis from our biryanis, our chow mein from our chao fan, there is rather less excuse for it.

The traditional, and still in many quarters rigidly followed, course was to abdicate any responsibility for choosing wine, and stick to beer instead. We are not out to rubbish this. The fact remains that, in the countries where the cooking styles discussed in this chapter originated, there is no tradition of European-type grape wine. Grapevines have indeed now been speculatively planted in India, China and Japan, and with some encouraging initial success, but they are very much a historically recent innovation, and inasmuch as alcohol was customarily drunk at all in the context of food, what was consumed was usually some form of rice product. The rice wines of Japan (saké) and China (shao-shing) are interesting drinks in themselves, but their flavour is nothing like that of grape wine. The nearest approximation to them for Westerners was to drink another grain-based product, wheat beer, examples of which were also to be found in these cuisines' native countries.

Lager-type beers such as India's Cobra, China's Tiger beer and Japan's Sapporo (there are of course many others) do work with the cooking of their respective countries, and we do not intend to deny that. However, we assume you're referring to this book because you are after something a little more challenging, and ultimately satisfying, than the fairly monotoned flavour of beer with your food. And the good news is that not only will wine quite commodiously accompany all the dishes enumerated in this chapter, but it makes a considerably more complex and gastronomically constructive match than beer. Nor do you need to confine yourself to the dreary purgatory of mediocre wine. You can profitably drink some very classy wines with many of these dishes, as we shall explain when we go through them.

We have dealt in this chapter with Indian, Chinese, Thai, Japanese and some other east Asian dishes, as well as some of the more popularly recognised cuisines of the Middle East and North Africa. Many of these modes get mixed and matched these days in that style of cooking known as Pacific Rim, to be found everywhere from Sydney to San Francisco. As this is a notably inventive, almost alchemical, approach to cooking, we can't hope to cover all possible manifestations of it, but in the sense that it has its roots in the national cuisines that are being discussed here, we hope you can use this chapter as a jumping-off point for wine ideas if you are eating in a restaurant that deals in this style of food.

Neither have we forgotten our vegetarian friends, who must have grown very tired in the past of turning to guides such as ours for help and inspiration, only to discover that it was meat and fish all the way, with only the dessert section proving to be of any practical use. Here, we have tried to list as many vegetarian main courses to be found on the more broad-minded menus of today as we can. We apologise in advance if any of your favourites are not here, but we have tried to give indications for as broad a range of basic ingredients and seasonings as possible, so that you have some pointers to work with.

In the bad old days, the difficulty for vegetarians and vegans lay in not knowing what additives had been used in wine to assist its clarification. Some of these are vegan-friendly (such as bentonite, a form of clay), others fine for lacto-vegetarian diets (such as egg white). Others, like gelatine, most definitely won't suit either. These days, happily (particularly in the high-street multiple outlets), this information is given on the back label, and there is a much greater range available of vegetarian and vegan wines to choose from. Look out for that information and, as with all less-than-precise ingredients listings, if in doubt, don't.

INDIAN

Starters
Bombay potatoes These sliced potatoes served in a spicy tomato dressing with onion work well with a good, fruity aperitif white. Sauvignon Blanc is, as ever, incomparable in this role, and it doesn't much matter where it comes from. Touraine, the upper Loire, Chile and South Africa will all suit, helping to get the digestive juices flowing with their bright, snappy acidity.

Lamb samosa A spiced mixture of minced lamb with vegetables wrapped in crisp gram-flour pastry, a lamb samosa will, as a red meat dish, take a soft, gentle red wine as its companion. Think Beaujolais Gamay (a simple

Beaujolais-Villages is just fine), or perhaps fruity Pinot Noir from Oregon or Burgundy's Côte Chalonnaise region (Mercurey or Givry). On the other hand, if you're apprehensive about serving or drinking red wine so early in a meal, choose one of the richer, spicier whites. Viognier from the south of France, Chile or Australia will fit the bill, as will Pinot Gris from Alsace, Oregon or New Zealand.

Onion bhaji These onion fritters, usually mixed with peas and carrot, are gently spiced and very moreish. They are fine with a relatively neutral white, but one with softness of texture rather than any overly bracing acidity. Alsace Pinot Blanc, Italian Pinot Grigio or Soave Classico, Spanish Viura, or blends such as Colombard-Chardonnay from Australia or South Africa, are good. If the bhajis are going to be dipped in a chillied-up, **tomato-based relish**, go for a correspondingly sharper white wine to accompany them. Chenin Blanc from South Africa or the Loire will be fine.

Shami kebab A fried lamb patty with a fair amount of forthright spicing, this needs a fittingly spicy red accompaniment. A peppery red from the northern Rhône (Crozes-Hermitage) or one of its counterparts from the southern sector (Vacqueyras), or a simple, unblended Shiraz from South Australia, are worthwhile bets.

Vegetable pakora/samosa The former are balls of mixed vegetables; the latter are more or less the same thing encased in batter. They usually incorporate peas, carrot, potato and sometimes lentils, and are gently spiced. They need a reasonably sharp-edged white wine to partner them, with more obvious fruit flavour than the wine you would choose to go with onion bhaji. Riesling is favourite, with the edgy, lime-tinged flavours of the Australian and New Zealand versions really coming into their own, but a dry (Trocken) or off-dry (Kabinett) example from either Germany or Austria will also do the trick.

Main Course Dishes

With Indian dishes, the sauce is most definitely the thing. You may want to modulate your wine choice a little, depending on whether the principal ingredient of the dish is chicken, lamb or king prawns, but as the ingredients of the sauce, and its degree of spicing, remain constant, it makes more sense to match the wine to those, as we have done here.

Bhuna An aromatic preparation that uses a lot of whole spices, without ending up overpoweringly hot, bhuna is happiest with an assertively spicy white. Gewürztraminer is a surefire bet, running the dish close for perfumed intensity. Alsace remains the source of the most concentrated examples, but there are also good ones now emerging from South Africa, Chile and New Zealand. If you find the flavour of Gewürz just a little too much of a good thing, try a Pinot Gris from Alsace, a Torrontes from Argentina or the little-known, and underrated, Irsai Oliver from the Czech Republic.

Biryani As biryani is a dry, rice-based dish without a sauce, and with gentle, sweetish spicing, it makes more sense than with other Indian main dishes to match the wine to the central ingredient. For a **king prawn biryani**, choose an astringent, moderately fruity white such as a Vouvray from the Loire, or one of its Chenin Blanc counterparts from the southern hemisphere (South Africa, New Zealand). With **chicken biryani**, go for a heavier, mellower-textured white, like a lightly oaked Chardonnay from Burgundy (Pouilly-Fuissé, St-Véran or even a barrel-matured Bourgogne Blanc), Australia, Chile, Argentina, Washington State or even Canada. For **lamb biryani**, a light red with zingy berry fruit flavours is best. Try Italy's Dolcetto or Barbera, one of the younger Valdepeñas reds of Spain, Australia's Tarrango or California's Gamay.

Butter chicken This is a notably fatty dish, mild in spicing, and made with large quantities of ghee, the clarified butter indispensable to the Indian culinary repertoire. You might think a nice buttery Chardonnay would be the perfect match but, while it certainly isn't a clash, it means that you end up with too great a similarity in texture between the wine and the food. Instead, look to one of the higher-acid, more sharply defined whites for a partner. A Muscadet de Sèvre-et-Maine with a couple of years' bottle-age is an appetising match for once, and so are the grassier Italian whites, such as Verdicchio, or similar Spanish whites such as those with a percentage of Verdejo in the blend (look to the northerly Rueda region to find those). Australia's Semillon, especially from the Hunter Valley, is a well-nigh unimprovable match, for the walnutty austerity of the flavours and its taut, disciplined texture on the palate.

Chicken saag A chicken dish made with spinach, and usually given assertive, chilli-hot spicing, this is a dish for the green, grassy whites. Spinach is in itself a highly acidic vegetable, and while its sharpness is certainly tamed in the cooking, you will nonetheless find that an acid-edged white is the best choice to stand up to it. Riesling is an obvious candidate, whether it be from Australia's Clare Valley, New Zealand's Marlborough region, or from northern Europe. The strong acid element in a youthful Alsace Riesling might prove a bit much, but one of the lighter German wines that retains a hint of residual sugar (look for Kabinett or Spätlese on the label), from the Pfalz, Rheingau or Mosel-Saar-Ruwer regions, would be stunning. Sauvignon would be the next best grape variety, from the upper Loire (e.g. Sancerre), South Africa or New Zealand.

Dhansak The sauce for this dish is thick and mealy, as it is made from a purée of brown lentils, while the spice level tends to be quite gentle. One of the oatmeally whites of Burgundy is a good bet, preferably made without too much (or any) oak. Chablis is a fine match, Chablis

premier cru an even better one. Chardonnays from southern Europe work well too, especially the new-wave wines
of Spain and Portugal, or else a lightly oaked example
from eastern Europe. The main principle seems to be to
avoid anything too fruity, so hold back on those Chilean,
Californian and New Zealand Chardonnays. Italy's whites
can be good here, particularly the silky-textured Soave
Classico, or try a Vernaccia di San Gimignano from
Tuscany. South Africa's Colombard, perhaps with some
Chardonnay in the blend, is also a sympathetic partner.

Jalfrezi A super-charged dish, with plenty of chilli heat,
as well as ginger and cinnamon noticeably in evidence,
jalfrezi is made with a tomato-based sauce and chunks of
red and green peppers. It is one of those dishes that
presents a stiff challenge to wine, but think acidity and
fruit rather than oak, and you'll get there. Sauvignon
Blanc is a good starting-point, from New Zealand,
Hungary, South Africa, Chile or the Loire. Inexpensive
Touraine Sauvignon is a great success, but a Pouilly-Fumé
at roughly twice the price won't come to any major grief.
Torrontes from Argentina is a star here too, for its bright
citrus intensity, and dry Rieslings from California,
Washington State or New Zealand also serve the purpose.

Kashmiri Anything served in the Kashmiri fashion tends
to be fruity, usually containing dried fruits such as
sultanas, and has a distinctly sweet edge, although
formulas vary quite widely. It seems best to choose a wine
with a definite quotient of residual sugar in the blend,
such as a Kabinett or Spätlese Riesling from the Mosel,
Pfalz or Nahe regions of Germany, or one of the higher-
alcohol examples from Austria. Another good bet, though
less of a star than Riesling, would be a Pinot Gris from
Alsace from one of the riper vintages.

Korma This sauce once enjoyed the reputation of being
everybody's first introduction to Indian cooking, having

some of the spice flavours, but without the palate-blasting heat of other dishes. It's a creamy, extremely gentle dish that should have a nutty backtaste from the use of almonds. Unoaked or very lightly oaked Chardonnay is such an obvious star performer here that it seems silly to look any further afield, especially when there are so many to choose from. Chile, central Europe, California, Oregon, Canada and Australia are the best, and the softly sour-creamy flavours of a reasonably mature Chablis (say, three years old) make a highly engaging match with a korma dish. If you have grown weary of Chardonnay lately (and we can't honestly blame you if you have), try an unoaked Viognier from Australia or Chile. The wines have more upfront fruit than Chardonnay, but this dish can easily cope with that.

Madras A hot, tomato-based sauce, Madras needs a wine with plenty of stuffing to stand up to it. This is one of those dishes that actually works better with a red wine than with a white. The softer textures of southern-hemisphere wines are best in this context, with Cabernet Sauvignon proving an unexpected winner. Chilean and Australian examples are particularly good, and the gentler tones of a Cabernet-Merlot blend from South Africa make a fine, appetising partnership. Unblended Merlots from Washington State, California and Chile will oblige, as will the rounded, plummy softness of a good Argentinian Malbec. Gigondas from the southern Rhône also gives a good account of itself. For an interesting change, and at the other end of the spectrum, a dry Muscat from Alsace makes an appealing partner for a Madras sauce.

Makhani This is a dish with a fair amount of dairy fat to it, usually from ghee, but many Indian restaurant versions use cream as well in the recipe, with the result that the spices are considerably gentler than in many other dishes. It doesn't need quite as sharp a wine as Butter Chicken, though, and some of those Chardonnays will work quite well (look to Australia's and Chile's unoaked, or the lighter burgundies, such as Rully). Lightly oaked white Rioja made in the modern style, perhaps entirely from the Viura grape variety, and some of the new generation of Portuguese whites from regions such as the Alentejo, are good partners for a makhani dish.

Pasanda Another fairly gently spiced dish, pasanda is both nutty (from the incorporation of almonds) and creamy (usually from yoghurt), and will benefit from a softly textured white with a nutty tinge on the finish. Good Chenin Blanc can have the requisite complexity, and an off-dry (demi-sec) version from the Loire, such as Vouvray or Montlouis, is a good choice. Pinot Blanc from Alsace or the United States has both the weight and the roundness, as do well-made examples of wine from the Cortese grape of northern Italy, such as Gavi. Otherwise, those lighter Chardonnays – see the entry on makhani above – once again demonstrate their versatility.

Phal Once thought strictly for those with a macho, competitive approach to Indian food, phal is the very hottest style of Indian dish available – hotter than vindaloo. Here, we really are going to suggest that, with so much chilli about, it scarcely matters what you drink as long as it is cold enough to refresh the mouth. High acidity is probably not a good idea, as it only emphasises the considerable pain that the palate is already undergoing. An Italian white with plenty of flavour-free Trebbiano in the blend seems favourite. In Tuscany, they make a wine called Galestro of absolutely no personality whatsoever. Lay in a couple of bottles of that, and then sally forth to the takeaway.

Rogan josh A tomato-based sauce with medium spice quotient, and classically made with lamb, rogan josh can make a good match with either a light red or a white wine. Among reds, Pinot Noir is the star team-mate, with wines from California or New Zealand showing particularly well.

Burgundy's Pinots tend to be just a little too acidic in their youth to make a really appealing marriage, but a Bourgogne rouge, or something like Côtes de Beaune-Villages, with three or four years in the bottle, should suffice. If white is the choice, one of the fruitier wines is favourite, to match the tomato: Sauvignons from Hungary, California or Chile, or one of the more obviously fruity Chardonnays (New Zealand, Chile or California), are good.

Tikka masala It has been said of late in the UK that chicken tikka masala has become the new staple national dish, so enormously popular has it become in both Indian restaurants and in ready-meal formats from the supermarket. The irony is that it isn't a true Indian dish at all, but one that was concocted (somewhat like chicken Kiev by the Russians) as a lure to Westerners seduced by the flavours of exotic seasonings. The boneless pieces of chicken are given a usually bright red spice rub, and are then served in a thickly creamy, even quite gloppy sauce. Made well, it is an appetising enough dish, and should be served with a white wine that has both its own creaminess and a cutting-edge of fresh, ripe acidity to complement the textures of the dish. Cool-climate Chardonnays are seemingly just made to fit this particular bill, with Chablis, the Casablanca region of Chile, the coastal areas of South Africa, Tasmania and New Zealand's South Island all showing their paces at this style.

Vindaloo Unfairly tarnished with the reputation of simply being the beer-boys' favourite way of ending an evening of single-minded indulgence, vindaloo is in fact an appetising and authentic dish of what was once the Portuguese area of India around Goa. The whole spices that go into it are ground in vinegar (originally wine vinegar), and the dish should properly contain chunks of potato (hence the 'aloo' part of its name). The sauce is indeed forthright with the burn of chopped chillies, and yet is balanced by the sweetness of tomatoes. White or red will suit it, if the wine is right.

White wines should be relatively gentle on the plate, with a fair amount of ripe fruit in them. Look to Riesling or Viognier for the right sort of balance. Rieslings from Australia or New Zealand, Viogniers from Chile or the south of France, are natural tablemates for vindaloo, and you could get way with one of the softer Sauvignon-Semillon blends of the Graves district of Bordeaux. For reds, keep it light and fruity, and you won't go far wrong. Pinot Noir from Chile, South Africa or Italy work well, as does the strawberryish ripeness of good cru Beaujolais (go for Fleurie or Brouilly). Italy's Barbera performs well, and Montepulciano d'Abruzzo from the Adriatic coast is a winner. Or recreate the (partially) Portuguese heritage of the dish with a Douro or Ribatejo red.

Xacutti This is more of a Sri Lankan (or, as it once was, Ceylonese) dish, and mobilises a more obviously tropical range of flavours, the most important of which is coconut. An exotically perfumed white is the optimum choice: go for Gewürztraminer from Alsace, Chile or Hungary, Torrontes from Argentina, Pinot Gris from Alsace, Washington State or Canada, or even a florally scented English white from a grape variety such as Bacchus or Reichensteiner.

CHINESE

Starters

Fishcake Battered fried fishcakes Chinese-style, usually made with squid, are an oily dish and, like many Chinese fried dishes, are best with a wine that has enough acidity to cut through the oil. Muscadet de Sèvre-et-Maine, young dry Vouvray, Chenin Blanc from South Africa or an English wine such as dry Ortega are all reasonably good matches, but avoid anything too fruity, which will appear to clash with the food.

Hot and sour soup Red chillies and lemon juice, respectively, provide the taste elements in the name of this popular soup, and present something of a challenge to wine. The best course is to opt for something delicate, but with enough bright fruit flavour to match the lemoniness. 'Riesling!' you will cry in unison, and we shan't disagree. Absolutely the best ones to match this soup come from Germany, where a slight natural grape sweetness in the wine will please the dish no end. The Mosel, Rheingau, Nahe and Pfalz are the best regions, and wines with Spätlese or even Auslese on the label will be the prime candidates. Failing that, a late-picked Riesling from California, Washington State or Australia will do well, but try to avoid any with alcohol above about 10%.

Peking duck Everybody's favourite DIY restaurant dish consists of these pancakes spread with plum sauce, and filled with cucumber threads, spring onions and bundles of shredded roast duck. The meat itself presents no problem, but the sweetness of the sauce rather throws a spanner in the works. Although we are dealing with red meat here, it's very much a white wine that's called for, and once again, one with a noticeable element of residual sugar on the palate. Kabinett and Spätlese Riesling from either Germany or Austria, late-picked Riesling or Muscat from the United States or Australia, demi-sec Vouvray from the Loire and even – if you're in the mood – demi-sec champagne are all good, as is one of those rosés, or blush wines, that has distinct residual sweetness. In fact, if the sugar level is properly restrained, and there is a certain amount of ripe raspberry fruit in the wine, that last suggestion is probably the best of all.

Salt-and-pepper squid These tentacles of squid deep-fried in a well-seasoned batter have become an increasingly popular dish in recent times. Like the fishcake listed opposite, they need a white wine with sharp acid definition to cut through the oiliness, and some spice tones to stand up to the black pepper. That sounds like a job for Austria's Grüner Veltliner, and indeed this austere, peppery white proves itself quite stunning in this context. Another possible route is Sauvignon, or perhaps better, a Sauvignon-Semillon blend from Australia, California or Bordeaux. In the last case, a simple Entre-deux-Mers would suffice, but choose one from the most recent vintage for the youthfully fresh acidity.

Spare ribs Roast mini-ribs of pork make a delightfully messy starter dish at a Chinese banquet, but as with the Peking duck, it's the bottled sauce they come coated in that sets the obstacle for a wine match. In the case of ribs, it's generally hoisin sauce (often referred to misleadingly on English-language Chinese menus as 'barbecue sauce'). No wine quite has the power to stand up to its sticky, savoury sweetness, but a lightly sweet white can sort of work. Reach again for those gently sweeter styles: late-picked Riesling and Muscat, demi-sec Chenin Blanc (Vouvray, Montlouis or Coteaux de l'Aubance).

Spring rolls Although two types of spring roll are usually listed on menus – one containing only vegetables such as carrot and beansprouts, the other with small prawns as well – the overall flavour is much the same, since it is dominated by the crisp batter that encases them. A dry white is the best option, again with a certain amount of acid bite to it. Chablis isn't a bad match, Sancerre possibly a better one. An unoaked, lemony Viura white from Rioja or Navarra works well, and so does the sappy flavour of cool-climate Chardonnay from coastal South Africa, Chile's Casablanca region, or from Tasmania.

Sweetcorn soup Either on its own, or with additions such as shreds of chicken or crab, sweetcorn naturally makes a fairly sweet-tasting, creamy-textured soup. One of the hot-climate Chardonnays, which can be relied on to have its own evident natural sweetness, is the best option. Australia, Chile's Central Valley, California and the inland regions of

South Africa such as Stellenbosch and Paarl, are all happy hunting-grounds for this style, and an Australian blend of Semillon and Chardonnay – never the most food-friendly of wines – suddenly makes a surprisingly well-behaved escort.

Dim Sum

No one wine can hope to make a satisfactory match with all the tasty little morsels that make up this Chinese approach to daytime eating. You will most likely be eating an array of deep-fried and steamed items, dumplings, fishcakes and bundles of rice, with varying levels of spice and sweetness. The fact that a fair few of the dishes are noticeably sweet suggests, however, that it is safest to stick to a delicately sweet white wine, such as late-picked Riesling or Muscat (Vendange Tardive is the designation for this style in Alsace, where the best matches are to be found), or demi-sec wines from the Loire (Vouvray or Anjou). If you are surrounded by Chinese families in a restaurant, you will certainly be the only person indulging in alcohol anyway, in which case it may well be better to stick to the tea for form's sake.

Main Courses

Black bean sauce The gentle note of savoury bitterness that the beans impart to this stir-fried mixture of meat with red and green peppers and onion makes it another dish that goes well with wines that have a delicate touch of their own sweetness, but don't overdo it. Hot-climate wines work well, whether it be Chardonnay, Semillon or Marsanne from Australia, Viognier from California or Chile, or one of those varietals made as a vin de pays d'Oc in the south of France. Those would be the choices if the meat in the dish is **pork or chicken**. If **beef** is used, a midweight red with a sweetly ripe edge can come into play. California's Zinfandel is just made for this role, and even one of the pink versions (confusingly labelled as White Zinfandel) can work, if you come across one that doesn't taste of boiled sweets.

Chicken and cashew nuts One of the perennial favourites of Chinese takeaway menus, this dish with its crunchy vegetables, nuts and usually a perceptible note of ginger, is a good background for almost any type of dry white wine, as long as it isn't too overwhelmingly fruity. Lightly oaked Chardonnay is, predictably enough, the winner, with the northerly wines of Burgundy (white Beaune and Santenay, for example) really shining, but warmer-climate Chardonnay from California, Australia or South Africa is fine too. Spanish and Portuguese whites, provided they are not too oaky, are good, and a very appetising match may be made with a dry sherry, either fino or manzanilla.

Chow mein These noodle dishes may comprise a mixture of meats and seafood (perhaps chicken, pork, duck and/or prawns, in the case of special chow mein), or may limit themselves to just chicken, along with crisp vegetable ingredients such as water chestnuts, bamboo shoots and carrots. The saucing in them tends to be light, even bland, and is barely more than a seasoning element, so that the choice of wine is wide indeed. It's best to stick with white, as a red would overwhelm, but within that parameter, the sky's the limit. Dry whites with a hint of nuttiness in the flavour work well, such as dry Chenin from the Loire, South Africa or New Zealand, Semillon from Australia's Hunter Valley, or an unoaked Burgundian Chardonnay (St-Véran or Chablis). Good Vinho Verde from Portugal, especially one with a little spritziness to it, at last attains some usefulness in the gastronomic context.

Crispy pork A piece of pork belly, roasted until the skin crisps up in the manner of British pork crackling, is one of the textural delights of the Chinese repertoire. It tends to be fatty too of course, and so some acidity in the accompanying wine is welcome. A light red can work unexpectedly well with this dish, with both Beaujolais (one of the lighter crus, such as Brouilly, Chiroubles or Juliénas) and Italy's Dolcetto coming through well. Otherwise, go with a fairly muscular white, like Chilean Chardonnay, Australian Marsanne or Verdelho, or California's Viognier, for their bright, citrussy personalities.

Duck with ginger and pineapple A stir-fried dish of usually pink-cooked duck breast with chunks of pineapple and threads of ginger root, this is a recipe that cries out for one of the lighter, sweet-fruited Zinfandels of California. Always a good choice with a fruity duck preparation, it is the precise composition of ripe red fruit and sweetish edge in the wine that helps it to accompany the food successfully. Dolcetto from Italy's Piedmont region makes the same sorts of noises, as – to a lesser degree – does the Veneto region's Valpolicella Classico. Rosé wines can succeed as well, especially if they have that gentle level of natural grape sweetness in them. Look to Argentina, Chile or Hungary for these.

Kung pao chicken Served in a chilli-hot sweet red sauce, this appetising chicken dish should also contain water chestnuts and peanuts for textural contrasts. Its combination of sweet and hot flavours sees us reaching for those lightly sweet Rieslings once more, with the chilli heat seeming to mandate higher alcohol than the German wines can boast. Austria, Alsace and Australia are the best sources. Ring the changes with alternative grape varieties such as Gewürztraminer, Pinot Gris or Muscat.

Lemon chicken These fried strips of battered chicken are served in an intensely lemony sauce, in which the sourness of the lemon juice is offset by considerable sweetness. Choose a wine with correspondingly sweet-and-sour flavours. The Gewürztraminer of Alsace, Germany, South Africa or New Zealand is a good flavour match, as it often contains a strong element of citrus (admittedly more like grapefruit than lemon, though). Australia's version of Verdelho is a nice match, and the Viogniers of southern

France and Chile work well. Incomparably best of all, though – and you'll just have to take our word for this – is to drink a sparing quantity of pale cream sherry with this dish. Too much and the two types of sweetness will simply become cloying, but a modest tot served well-chilled makes an improbably sublime match for such a generally despised style of fortified wine.

Steamed fish One of the simplest and most satisfying of all Chinese dishes is a piece of white fish (classically sea bass or skate) cooked in a steamer with shredded ginger and spring onions. It wants a delicate, dry white to go with it, with unoaked Chardonnay and Riesling being once again the top choices. Simple Chablis is brilliant – and better than a *premier cru* wine, in fact – and the drier versions of Riesling from Alsace, New Zealand, Austria or California are pretty wonderful too. Southern European whites are very good as well, with Italy's Vernaccia di San Gimignano and Albana di Romagna both acquitting themselves impressively.

Sweet-and-sour The sauce in these dishes is the main hurdle for wine to leap over. It barely matters whether the principal ingredient is battered pork or chicken, or king prawns. Pineapple, red peppers and carrots provide the sweetness, while vinegar adds the just-noticeable sour note. Go for sweetness in the wine, and keep it white. Late-picked Gewürztraminer from Alsace, Germany or Washington State, Auslese Rieslings from Austria or Germany, even one of the lesser-known sweet whites of southwest France, such as Monbazillac or Saussignac, are the kinds of lines to think along. A small glass of well-chilled white port, not a wine that finds much favour otherwise, comes through with flying colours.

Szechuan beef Sizzling dishes from the west of China are usually highly spiced, containing the famous Szechuan peppercorns with ginger and chilli. Bitter-skinned green pepper is another favoured ingredient, making a beef version of this style of cooking one of the few Chinese dishes that can stand up unequivocally to a red wine, and a pretty spicy one at that. Northern Rhône Syrah is a good bet, with both Cornas and Crozes-Hermitage showing well, but Grenache-based southern Rhône blends are not far behind. Try a Vacqueyras or Lirac. Portugal's Periquita grape variety, with its liquoricey, peppery strains, makes an unusual but successful match, and good things happen when California's Syrah, Australia's Shiraz and one of the riper, softer versions of South Africa's Pinotage are paired with Szechuan beef.

THAI

Starters

Chicken satay Chicken meat on a stick coated in a delicately sweet peanut sauce, satay has reached that level of recognition that qualifies it as a truly international dish. A dryish white wine with a little acidity but not too much vivid fruit is what it needs to partner it. Australian Semillon, from the Hunter Valley particularly, is a good choice, as are the dry whites of northern Spain and Portugal (look out for a grape variety called Fernão Pires from the latter country). Soave makes a happily precise match, and so – you guessed it – do our old friends, unoaked and lightly oaked Chardonnay. A central or eastern European example seems to have the exact weight for the dish.

   Fishcakes Thai fishcakes are fairly similar to the Chinese version, being small, battered pieces of white fish, often squid, but traditionally served with a red-hot, sweet chilli dipping sauce. It's the sauce that scares off most wines, and in this context, it really is best to keep it plain and simple. Everyday *vin de pays* French white blends with crisp acidity will do, whether from the pays de Gascogne in the southwest, or perhaps the pays Nantais in the Loire

Valley. Straightforward Italian whites can be fine too, with the demi-sec (or *abboccato*) version of Umbria's Orvieto performing well. Otherwise, Colombard-Chardonnay blends from South Africa or Australia will suit.

Noodle salad Prawns and chicken form the centrepiece of the traditional Thai noodle salad, alongside those very thin noodles and plenty of sharp, pungent seasoning, majoring on lime juice. It's a dish for sharp, fruity white wines, principally Sauvignon Blanc or Riesling. Look to Sancerre, Menetou-Salon or Quincy in the upper Loire, South Africa or Chile for the Sauvignons, while the lime-leaf edge of Australian or New Zealand Riesling is a very fitting match with the seasonings in the dish.

Squid salad Dressed to impress with lemongrass, lime leaves and coriander, the appetisingly sour flavours of squid salad are offset by the strong burn of chilli, calling for a dry white with firm fruit. On the principle of fighting fire with fire, it's best to go for a wine that has fairly assertive acidity of its own. Cool-climate Sauvignons are a fine match, whether from New Zealand or the Loire, or northern Burgundy's Sauvignon de St-Bris. Another oddball Burgundy appellation is Bourgogne Aligoté, producing white wines with pronounced lemony acidity and a touch of spritz. One of these, especially from the village of Bouzeron, would make a good partner for this dish.

Tom yum soup This spicy broth is usually red-hot with chillies and sour with lemon and lime flavours, and contains prawns, mushrooms and lemongrass. It is probably best taken on its own, but if you do fancy drinking something alongside it, try a glass of well-chilled manzanilla sherry, the bracing, salty tang of which will stand it in good stead.

Main Courses
Beef in peanut sauce A curried dish flavoured with peanuts, coconut and chilli, this is a dish that works well, as not many

Thai dishes do, with a soft-centred red. A southern Rhône blend such as one of the Côtes du Rhône-Villages wines that has a specific village name appended to it (e.g. Chusclan, Sablet or Cairanne) will fit the bill, as would a Grenache-Shiraz blend from South Australia. A Loire Cabernet Franc such as Bourgueil or Chinon, with its nippy, redcurranty acidity, isn't bad either, especially from one of the riper vintages, and Pinot Noir with a bit of oak-ageing on it to round it out is also fine. Go for a Californian, Australian or New Zealand example of the latter.

Green chicken curry This creamy-sauced curry dish, made with Thai basil, lime leaves, lemongrass and galangal, incorporates green beans as well as chicken. It is the kind of dish that is just shouting out for Sauvignon Blanc to accompany it, and one of the fruitier, riper New Zealand versions is just right. Look to the Marlborough region for the best match. An oak-aged Sauvignon, perhaps from California, or an oaked Sauvignon-Semillon blend from Bordeaux or Western Australia, also come into their own here. Pinot Gris from Alsace, with its slight hint of residual sweetness and musky spice, makes another appealing partnership.

Noodles and beansprouts A sharply flavoured combination of crunchy textures, this everyday dish works well with a white wine with sharply etched acidity, but quite neutral flavours. Frascati or Soave from Italy are good with it, and so is the perennial neutral dry white, Muscadet de Sèvre-et-Maine. Pinot Gris from Oregon, or northern Italy's Pinot Grigio (the latter now available in an appetising sparkling version), are reasonable matches too.

Red curry A medium-hot dish with plenty of assertive spicing in the shape of lime leaves, ginger and chilli, given distinct pungency by the use of the fermented Thai fish sauce, *nam pla*, red curry needs a forthright, spicy white to do it justice. Gewürztraminer, which can be distinctly gingery in itself, is a surefire choice for grape variety (Alsace,

New Zealand or South Africa), and so is the spice-scented Viognier (Chile, southern France or Australia). Austria's Grüner Veltliner once again shows its mettle, as does the florally perfumed Torrontes of Argentina. Or try a Rias Baixas from the Galicia region of northwest Spain, made from the native Albariño grape.

Special Thai noodles If comparison is useful, this is a little like a Thai version of China's special chow mein, with both meat and seafood combining in a crunchy-textured noodle dish full of salty, piquant seasonings. A summer-fruited pink wine is a good match for the prawns in the dish. Cabernet Sauvignon rosés from Chile, Argentina or Hungary certainly come into their own, as do some of the spicier rosés of southern France, particularly Corbières. If you prefer to stick with white, choose a dry but fruity specimen. Sauvignon is as good as ever in this style (think Loire or South Africa), but the fruitier versions of Chardonnay are useful too (Chile, New Zealand or California). If opting for Chardonnay, avoid any heavily oaked wines.

Stir-fried pork Pork strips stir-fried with sweet basil and chilli require a forthrightly flavoured dry white with some stuffing to match the heat. Pinot Gris, Gewürztraminer and even Muscat from Alsace are all smart matches, dry Chenin from South Africa or the Touraine district of the Loire (Vouvray or Montlouis) is good, or look – yet again – to Sauvignon Blanc in the flinty, high-acid style of the upper Loire (Sancerre or Pouilly-Fumé) or the cooler coastal regions of South Africa (such as Swartland). If wine, for some unfathomable reason, doesn't appeal, this is one of those dishes that works well enough with a glass of cold Singha Thai beer.

Stir-fried squid Squid wok-fried with ginger, garlic and fish sauce is a pungently flavoured dish that will benefit from a similarly tasting grape variety. The Sylvaner of Alsace is a promising match, also appearing in Germany's

Frankenwein, and some of the less highly regarded varieties of German wine, such as Müller-Thurgau (once widely grown in New Zealand too), suddenly taste rather classy. If those prove hard to find, go with a South African, New Zealand or California dry Chenin Blanc, or even a very lightly oaked Chardonnay from Bulgaria. Bourgogne Aligoté is worth considering too, if you see it.

JAPANESE

The traditional accompaniment to Japanese food is of course saké, the fermented rice wine that has its ardent connoisseurs just as grape wine does. Served either cold or slightly warm, saké is indeed a good match with some dishes, although by no means all. It is anyway a considerably more sympathetic partner than the heavily watered Scotch or Japanese whisky drunk by Japanese businessmen with their food. The following suggestions will point you in the direction of the grape, should you decide to avail yourself of the often very fine wine lists offered in Japanese restaurants.

Gyoza These light dumplings of minced pork are fairly bland in flavour, and need only the gentlest, most neutrally flavoured wine to go with them. Cue the unoaked Chardonnay. Almost any source will do, but the pole position is probably jointly occupied by unoaked Australian Chardonnay and simple Chablis.

Miso soup The sharply acidic seasonings in this thin soup, which often contains shiitake mushrooms and spring onions, are sufficiently expressive to need only the most neutral background in an accompanying wine. A tot of dry fino sherry scores on two counts: it has the right dry flavour to match the soup, and the smaller quantity in which it is served, compared to an unfortified table wine, ensures that you aren't coping with too liquid a combination.

Sashimi Pieces of raw fish, very lightly if at all seasoned, and often presented on clumps of glutinous rice, must not be outdone by any wine they are teamed with. The exemplary freshness of the fish is what this dish is all about. Light, unoaked whites with gentle acidity are best. Go to Spain or Italy for the likes of Albariño or Trebbiano wines of the most recent vintage, or opt for a Colombard from either Australia or South Africa. A light, Brut-style blanc de blancs champagne isn't a bad flavour match, but as so often, the bubbles get in the way if drunk in quantity.

Soba noodles A dish of buckwheat noodles, usually containing crisp vegetable strands and perhaps some pickled ginger, this is best with fairly bland whites with light acidity – the subtle background approach once more. Alsace Pinot Blanc, Soave Classico, unoaked white Rioja, or a Pinot Gris from Oregon or New Zealand will all come up trumps.

Sushi rolls These are made up of raw fish wrapped in nori (seaweed), seasoned with wasabi (similar to horseradish) and ginger. The wasabi contributes the same kind of heat as chilli does in other contexts, and consequently a spicy white with pronounced acidity is best. Viognier varietals from California, Chile or southern France make a fashionable marriage, but Grüner Veltliner from Austria should not be forgotten, and a vigorously chilled, basic Chablis is fine too. Some of the more perfumed white varieties of Portugal (such as the flowery Roupeiro) are worth trying as well.

Tempura Deep-fried tempura, in its subliminally light batter, has proved one of the most readily translatable Japanese dishes for western palates. **Tempura-battered prawns** are good with delicate Sauvignons from the Loire or South Africa, or perhaps a good Muscadet de Sèvre-et-Maine with the words *sur lie* on the label. For **tempura-battered vegetables**, depending on what they are, a slightly weightier wine can be tried. Lightly oaky Chardonnays from Chile, central Europe or southern France will all serve.

Teriyaki This savoury brown sauce is applied to red

meats such as beef or duck. It isn't particularly spicy, but there is a sour edge in it that the wine needs to take into account. Gentle reds such as Italian Barbera and Aglianico del Vulture, Spain's Valdepeñas Reserva, simple Bourgogne rouge Pinot Noir, or Australian Tarrango forge successful alliances with the food, and even one of the lighter red Zinfandels of California can work. Or try a Syrah rosé from Argentina or Australia.

MIDDLE EASTERN AND NORTH AFRICAN

Couscous The ingredients in Morocco's staple dish vary hugely from one restaurant to the next. A mainstream version might be expected to contain peppers, onion, dried fruit, and some gentle spicing along the lines of cumin and pepper, along with the grains themselves. It tends to err on the side of blandness, if anything, and needs a correspondingly subtle wine to go with it, although the good news is that it doesn't much matter whether it's red or white. A soft-toned Moroccan red, such as a Cabernet Sauvignon, which often has more than a hint of raisin in the flavour, would be an ethnically unimpeachable choice, while the light spiciness of a Lebanese pink (usually to be found on the wine list in the kind of restaurant that serves couscous) is also worth considering. For whites, light and neutral seems best (head towards unoaked Chardonnay or the likes of Alsace Pinot Blanc or Italian Pinot Grigio), although a simple Touraine Sauvignon won't upset the applecart.

Felafel This Lebanese street food, a spicy pastry wrap of chickpeas flavoured with cumin, hardly requires that you have a glass of wine in the other hand as you perambulate through the street market eating one. That said, they do crop up on restaurant menus as a starter, and are best paired with a sharply flavoured southern European or eastern Mediterranean white. Greece's Rhoditis grape variety is a good bet, as are the Verdejo of northern Spain and the Bical of Portugal.

Kebabs What do you want in your kebab? If **spiced meat** is the morsel of choice, as it tends to be, go with an oily red of the Spanish or Portuguese type (old-school Rioja Crianza or Valdepeñas from the former, Dão or Bairrada from the latter). For a slightly more upmarket version, made with king prawns, choose a sappy white with some class: good Rieslings and Sauvignons are best.

Merguez These thin Lebanese lamb sausages spiced with cumin and paprika are richly flavoured and quite fatty. Pair them with a full-bodied, robustly peppery red with unabashed acidity and moderate tannins. Northern Rhône Syrah such as St-Joseph, Crozes-Hermitage or Cornas are all great with merguez, and so are their Syrah/Shiraz equivalents from California, South Africa and Australia's Barossa Valley. The last tends to have a distinct topnote of mint, which matches the lamb in the sausages to perfection.

Tabbouleh A grain salad made with bulgur (cracked wheat), lightly spiced, tabbouleh makes an appetising starter dish with a glass of vigorously chilled Sauvignon Blanc. Best in this context come from South Africa, the upper Loire (Sancerre, Menetou-Salon) or Chile. Alternatively, a Chenin or Riesling from northern Europe has the right amount of acid grip (try one of the dry German wines labelled Trocken). A Lebanese white, if there's one on the list, would be an impeccable way of entering into the spirit of the thing.

VEGETARIAN

Cauliflower gratin Many people like to eat this baked dish of cauliflower florets cooked in a rich cheese sauce as a main dish, rather than as an accompaniment. The Cheddar and/or Gruyère in the sauce call for a fairly robustly constituted red wine. Italy's Nebbiolo specialities, Barolo and Barbaresco, are quite capable of blending in obligingly with the dish, as are Spain's Ribera del Duero, Portugal's Douro reds, and the likes of Shiraz and Shiraz-Cabernet blends from Australia, Grenache-Syrah blends from California, and smooth-contoured Reserve Merlot from Chile.

Melanzane alla parmigiana A classic Italian dish that consists of sliced aubergine baked under a bubbling cheesy layer, this needs a midweight Italian red to partner it. Ripe Chianti Classico or Chianti Rufina, Rosso di Montalcino, and Vino Nobile di Montepulciano, all from Tuscany, Tempranillo-based blends from Navarra, Portugal's Alentejo reds, and Italian varietals from the Americas, such as Bonarda from Argentina or Sangiovese from California, are the ways to go.

Nut roast The earthy tones of a textbook nut roast, sliced hot from the oven, suggest a nutty-flavoured, fairly rich white wine. Lightly oaky Chardonnay is great, especially from the middle region of Burgundy, the Côte Chalonnaise (Rully or Montagny, for instance). Semillon from New South Wales or Washington State makes a big, strapping partner, and Alsace Pinot Blanc has the right amount of fat. Reds work too, as long as they are not too tannic. A Côtes du Rhône-Villages, or Grenache-based blend from Australia, California or South Africa, will all do fine.

Oeufs en cocotte Virtually no egg dish is more comforting than whole eggs baked in little ramekins on top, perhaps, of a layer of creamy mushrooms. The richest styles of Chardonnay go beautifully with this dish. Indeed, if you think it's appropriate, or somebody is willing to treat you on your birthday, the savoury, oaky magnificence of Puligny-Montrachet, or similar Reserve Chardonnays from California, Australia, New Zealand or Chile, would be superb. Lower down the financial scale, Rhône whites make a fittingly rich-textured, but neutrally flavoured, match. White Côtes du Rhône-Villages (or, flying high again, white Châteauneuf-du-Pape or white Hermitage) is appetising with baked eggs.

Ratatouille Originating in Provence, this baked dish of aubergine, courgettes, peppers, tomatoes and onions justly demands a Provençal wine to accompany it. The trickiness in finding a match lies in the abundance of fresh herbs there should be in the dish (basil, oregano, marjoram and so forth). Bandol is a highly attractive red from the region, and a reasonably mature one (with at least four years in the bottle) will partner ratatouille well. On the other hand, you may feel that the tomato in the dish is better with a fruit-filled, moderately acid white such as a Sauvignon from Chile, New Zealand, Hungary or the Loire (simple Touraine Sauvignon can be stunning with ratatouille). The choice is yours.

Spanish omelette A straightforward omelette, as opposed to tortilla, comprising a mixture of peppers, tomato and onion (and perhaps also potato) in a garlicky egg mixture needs a Spanish white. Viura varietals from Rioja and Navarra, wines from Rueda that have some Sauvignon in the blend, and Albariño from Galicia are all fine, as are the otherwise personality-free whites of central Spain made from the widely planted Airen grape variety.

Stuffed mushrooms Upturned mushrooms filled with a garlicky breadcrumb mixture seasoned with parsley and other herbs call very strongly for a red wine partner. Keep it soft and light, though: Barbera from northern Italy, southern Rhône blends, or Gamay from California or Beaujolais (Chiroubles, Brouilly or Beaujolais-Villages), will all answer the call.

Stuffed peppers These whole peppers are either baked or poached, and filled with a lightly spiced rice and vegetable mixture. Green peppers need either a lightish red such as a Beaujolais, Italian Dolcetto or simple Pinot Noir from Chile or eastern Europe, or a vegetally flavoured white such as Alsace Sylvaner or Chablis. The red variety are definitely happier with a white wine that has a little residual sweetness in it, like German or Austrian Kabinett or Spätlese Riesling, or an Alsace Pinot Gris.

Vegetable moussaka This veggie version of moussaka is made in much the same way as traditional moussaka, except that instead of the minced lamb, it uses green lentils to imitate the texture of the meat, and add a certain earthiness to the flavour. Reds are definitely best, with Greek Nemea, Salice Salentino from Italy's Puglia region, Australia's Grenache and California's Pinot Noir all showing up well.

Vegetable terrine A slice of brightly flavoured (and coloured) vegetable terrine makes a palate-cleansing way to start a meal. In recent years, the fashionable touch has been to wrap the outside of it with green leek to replace the bacon in a meat-based terrine. A pairing with Chilean or southern French Viognier gives the palate plenty to think about, and the fruitiness of New Zealand and Californian Chardonnay also add greatly to the appeal of the dish.

10

DESSERTS

More than with any other food category, the business of finding wines to go with desserts requires a formidable level of precision. Most savoury dishes will tolerate a rough-and-ready approach to wine matching, whether the issue is strong seasonings, hot spices or just forthrightly flavoured main ingredients. With desserts, though, the main factor to consider is sweetness, but that turns out to be the most demanding taste type of all to please. Too dry a wine will end up tasting mean and sour, while an overly sweet one will simply overwhelm the food, becoming a sort of substitute dessert in itself.

The paradox is that it is just here, nearing the finishing line of a multi-course dinner, that most people tend to take their eye off the ball with the wine. The assumption tends to be that any sticky old thing will do, or – worse still – that a dry sparkler, classically champagne, will add to the overall air of gaiety and indulgence. That latter habit does seem to be on the wane, and with any luck, the days of drinking dry champagne with gooey gâteaux will soon be behind us. It is a particular torment as this is the only context in which either of us can ever be heard to turn down the offer of a glass of champagne, a moment guaranteed to evoke the agonies of the damned.

With the richest and creamiest desserts, only the richest and creamiest dessert wines will suffice, but lighter dishes, such as fruit salads, tarts and mousses, would be completely steamrollered by such wines. That is because the level of sweetness in them isn't just a matter of flavour, but of texture too. Depending on the winemaking method, a very sweet wine, such as one affected by botrytis, the so-called noble rot that shrivels the grapes on the vine, concentrating the sugar levels in them as the water content goes down, will generally have much too thick and viscous a feel in the mouth to sit discreetly alongside the airy, eggy texture of a mousse. Then again, the much more densely eggy texture of a crème brûlée absolutely demands it.

The other point to bear in mind when considering whether to lay on a dessert wine for your guests is that most of the decent ones are forbiddingly expensive, on account of the labour-intensive procedures involved in growing and vinifying them. There are reasonably priced sweet wines (and we have recommended some in the following pages), but their flavours tend to be fairly one-dimensional, and they consequently have only a limited range of applications on the dinner table. In other words, if you are going to economise, this is the stage of the meal at which to do it. People often appreciate an alcohol breather, and you may well be going on to serve a fortified or table wine with the cheeses (this assumes that you are having pudding before cheese in the Anglo-American fashion, and not the other way around, as the Europeans do). The good news, if you do decide to serve a dessert wine, is that a little goes a long way, and many of the most opulent dessert wines are available in half-bottles. Similarly, most good restaurant wine lists will offer dessert wine by the glass. The mark-up may well be horrific, but at least it represents a way of tasting a sweet wine with your dessert without overloading the system with too much more alcohol.

Some wine commentators go as far as to announce that the whole business of drinking sweet wines with desserts is the work of barbarians. Our opinion is that that is arrogant twaddle, but it is undoubtedly the case that many sweet wines also go well with certain types of cheese. For these matches, see Chapter 11. By the same token, there are some types of dessert that really don't need an accompanying wine at all, and we have listed those below too, with some explanation as to why not.

Apple pie An ordinary **English-style apple pie**, made with Bramley apples in shortcrust pastry, needs a surprisingly sweet wine to accompany it, for all that the pie filling might be quite tart. The botrytised (noble-rotted) versions of Chenin Blanc from the Loire are very good with it (look for Coteaux du Layon or Quarts de Chaume). Botrytised Chenins from elsewhere will also work, though, and may be kinder on the pocket. If the pie is made in the **Dutch or German style**, and contains raisins and a seasoning of cinnamon, a rotted version of one of the Alsace varieties will echo the flavour of the sweet spice. Choose a Gewürztraminer or Pinot Gris: labelled Sélection de Grains Nobles from Alsace, or Beerenauslese from Germany or Austria.

Apple strudel This Germanic dessert requires a sweet wine of that provenance to do it full justice. A German or Austrian rotted Riesling of the Beerenauslese category is the best choice. If sweet enough, a Riesling Eiswein, which tends to have lower alcohol, may be just as good, with its lighter texture reflecting the papery delicacy of the strudel pastry.

Baked Alaska The dessert that seems a contradiction in terms, meringue- and sponge-encased ice-cream that is briefly done in the oven, is such a bizarre composition of flavours and textures that it is quite difficult to find a wine that will go with it, especially as (see below) wines don't generally perform well with ice-cream. About the best bet is a simple Asti or Moscato Spumante, or its French equivalent Clairette de Die Tradition, which must contain at least 50% Muscat/Moscato.

Baked apple A dessert apple transformed to woolly sweetness by baking with brown sugar, usually with raisins packed into the cavity created by coring it, and often served with custard (crème anglaise), is best with a fairly full, syrupy wine, such as a Coteaux du Layon from the Loire, Sauternes from Bordeaux, an Austrian Trockenbeerenauslese or a Canadian Icewine.

Baked banana Baked in its split skin with demerara sugar and a little sweet spice, the rich fattiness of banana demands a strikingly rich and intensely sweet dessert wine. High alcohol helps too, so go for the likes of Sauternes, Muscat de Beaumes-de-Venise, botrytised Semillon from Australia or an Italian vin santo.

Banoffee pie The colossally rich combination of banana and toffee on a buttery pastry base was invented at a Sussex restaurant in 1972, and will need your richest and strongest dessert wines. Muscat de Beaumes-de-Venise works very well, because the orangey hint in its flavour helps to slice through the richness of the dish, while the fortified strength of the wine stands up to its envelopingly gooey texture. Australian Orange Muscat and Flora, though lower in alcohol, works reasonably well, as do the Trockenbeerenauslese wines of Austria, and the Icewines of Canada, made from grape varieties such as Vidal or Bouvier.

Bavarois Known as Bavarian cream to Americans, the bavarois is a set mixture of fruit purée, whipped cream, sugar and usually a little gelatine to set, and is not to be confused with a mousse, which relies on beaten egg-white to set it. The bavarois is a little creamier and richer than a mousse, and is often served with a matching fruit coulis. Late-picked Rieslings and Muscats match it best for texture and sweetness, whether they come from Alsace (Vendange Tardive), Washington State, California or Australia. A German Eiswein Riesling, picked when the grapes have frozen on the vines in the dead of winter, is another good choice.

Bread-and-butter pudding This once-humble British leftovers dish was once little more than slices of old bread baked in custard with a few raisins or sultanas scattered in. Haute cuisine trendiness has now bestowed a sheen of *grande luxe* on it. The bread is often fresh brioche, the custard is made with thick cream and real vanilla, and it often has a bubbling glaze of apricot jam on top. In this latter state, it feels as though it would turn up its nose at anything less than classed-growth Sauternes, and certainly that is a rather delicious match. If the budget doesn't run to it, try one of the lesser-known French blends of botrytised Semillon and Sauvignon, such as Monbazillac or Saussignac, or go to Australia or California for unblended rotted Semillon.

Cheesecake Traditional German **baked cheesecake** on a softly crumbly biscuit base is a densely rich, though plainly flavoured, dish. It isn't bad with the sweetest styles of German wine (Beerenauslese and Trockenbeerenauslese), made from Riesling or one of the lesser-known grapes such as Scheurebe or Kerner. Australia's Orange Muscat and Flora probably slightly outdoes that match, though, for the extra stuffing it has. A **fruit-topped cheesecake**, made with cream cheese but set with gelatine rather than baked, and based on a crunchier biscuit underlay, needs a sweet wine with noticeably higher acidity. Alsace Riesling Sélection de Grins Nobles, or a botrytised Chenin from the Loire, such as Bonnezeaux or Coteaux du Layon, are particularly good.

Chocolate brownies These slabs of cake with their slightly brittle texture were once eaten as a mid-morning snack with coffee, but have been imported on to the dessert menu in many restaurants, where they may be accompanied by ice-cream or a syrupy sauce. On their own, they are good with the fortified Muscats of southern France (Beaumes-de-Venise, Frontignan or St-Jean-de-Minervois), or one of the sweet wines of Jurançon in the deep southwest. Late-picked Muscats from California fare almost as well.

Chocolate fondant Otherwise known as chocolate moelleux, this is a baked chocolate sponge with a hollow centre filled with extremely rich molten dark chocolate. Only a rotted wine has the weight and concentration to deal with it, so go for botrytised Semillon or Riesling from Australia, the same from California, or a Sauternes.

Chocolate marquise A marquise is a sort of chocolate terrine, set in a loaf-tin, and composed of rich dark chocolate mixed with eggs and butter to a state of silky smoothness. As with many chocolate creations, it is best partnered with a sweet Muscat wine with fairly high alcohol. Muscat de Beaumes-de-Venise is good, as is another, less widely seen fortified wine, Setúbal Moscatel from western Portugal. The grapey edge of acidity in these wines is what helps them to compete with the richness of both flavour and texture in the dish.

Chocolate mousse The classic chocolate mousse consists of nothing other than chocolate, eggs and sugar, but some versions add butter, and others include a dash of black coffee to broaden the flavour. Once again, Muscat is its best friend, but you can get away with a lighter version than fortified Muscat if you so choose. Vendange Tardive Muscat from Alsace or Washington State late-picked Muscat are both fine, as is the sweet Orange Muscat of certain Californian producers.

Chocolate soufflé The lightest chocolate dish of all, a soufflé requires a correspondingly delicate dessert wine to partner it. German Beerenauslese wines made from Pinot Gris (called Grauburgunder or Ruländer there) or Gewürztraminer are good, as is the simple style of late-picked Muscat produced in Australia and California.

Christmas pudding Absolutely the best possible choice to go with the traditional suety, dense Christmas pudding is Asti, the sparkling Moscato wine made in Italy's Piedmont region. Its low alcohol, grapey frothiness and squeaky-clean flavour are just the ticket at the end of what has always inevitably been a digestively challenging meal. Moscato Spumante, which is a slightly cheaper but very similar version of the same thing, is almost equally good, or you might try a Moscato d'Asti, which is a virtually still version with an alcohol level more usually suited to beer than wine. Anything else will seem too heavy and cloying.

Crème brûlée This classic French dessert is nothing more than a set mixture of egg yolks, sugar and cream, with a brittle, caramelised, brown sugar top, but it has become almost obsessively fashionable. These days, it is often given some extraneous flavour addition, such as red fruits, nuts, chocolate, even savoury herbs, but for the traditional recipe, a creamy, cask-aged Sauternes is the Number One match. The custardy flavours of botrytised Semillon are a godsend with anything eggy and creamy, and if the wine has a flash of sharpening acidity from the inclusion of Sauvignon Blanc, then so much the better. A reasonably fresh Tokaji from Hungary, provided that it is one of the sweeter ones (look for the designation 5 Puttonyos on the label) can work well, and so can the rotted Semillon and even Riesling dessert wines of Australia.

Crème caramel This featherlight, eggy dessert in its dark brown, thin caramel sauce would be totally overwhelmed by anything as heavy as Sauternes. Very delicate late-picked

Rieslings, such as Beerenauslese wines from the Mosel region of Germany, are OK. Late-picked Muscats from California would be the next best bet, but this is a dish that isn't truly happy with any particular wine.

Crêpes suzette A classic of the French *haute cuisine* repertoire, these are sweet pancakes made with orange liqueur, very often flamed at the table in the gourmet restaurants of an earlier era. They have melted butter poured over them too, and so, although light-textured, the cumulative impact of the dish is quite rich. Fortified Muscat, with its orangey flavour, once again comes up trumps, with Muscat de Beaumes-de-Venise leading the pack. Californian Orange Muscat works, although it is distinctly more delicate, and so does the Sélection de Grains Nobles version of Alsace Muscat. Or you could simply drink a little glass of chilled Cointreau or Grand Marnier.

Egg custard tart A traditional British dish that is probably overdue for a revival in times when all the other puddings of our childhood have staged comebacks, the light, nutmeg-sprinkled, eggy filling of a custard tart goes quite well with a Vouvray moelleux from the Loire (that's the style that's a bit sweeter again than a demi-sec). Sweet Ste-Croix-du-Mont from southwest France, not far from Sauternes and enjoying a hint of its reflected glory, is also a canny choice, if you come across it.

Fruit crumbles Depending on the fruit used, a baked crumble usually has a noticeably tart edge to the fruit filling, the juices of which should come seeping appetisingly through the buttery, floury topping. **Gooseberry or rhubarb** crumbles need a wine with a definite line of bright acidity woven through it. Those rotted Chenin Blanc wines from the Loire are favourites (Quarts de Chaume, Coteaux du Layon), but the less syrupy, but still sweet, versions of Anjou Blanc will work too. With a **plum** crumble, you can get away with something a little less acidic. A Monbazillac or Loupiac from near Bordeaux, or a late-picked Muscat or Riesling from Washington State, will fit the bill.

Fruit salads It is very hard to generalise about drinking wine with fruit salads as there are so many variables. Firstly, there is the question of which varieties are used. There is a world of difference between an old-fashioned peach, pear, apple and cherry assemblage and one that is filled with tropical fruits such as mango, papaya, aromatic melon and passion-fruit. Most fresh fruits have the kind of acidity that clashes disturbingly with wine, and so the next question will be what they are dressed in. How sweet is that syrup? And is it a neutral sugar syrup, or is it flavoured with citrus juices, and maybe sweet spices such as cinnamon or ginger? If in doubt, serve no wine, but just let the flavours of the ripe, fresh fruits speak for themselves (a particularly clever strategy if you are serving the seasonal soft fruits of summer). If you insist, a light, late-picked Muscat from California shouldn't come to much harm, and some English sweet wines, from grape varieties such as Huxelrebe, have the right kind of elder-flowery charm (though not with exotic fruits). Otherwise, hang on and have some more wine with the cheeses.

Fruit soufflés Keep it light and fresh with a baked fruit soufflé. Late-picked Muscats, Rieslings and Gewürz-traminers from California, Germany (Beerenauslese) or Alsace (Vendange Tardive) are good, as are Italy's Moscato d'Asti and sparkling Asti, and Clairette de Die Tradition from eastern France.

Fruit tarts Of the different kinds of fruit tart, the ones based on short pastry, with glazed sliced fruits on a layer of ground-almond **frangipane**, are probably the most popular. They require a wine that's a bit sweeter than the average late-picked specimen, and yet not quite as sweet as a fully botrytised one. Austrian Beerenauslese, or the sweet category unique to Austria's wine regulations, Ausbruch, are both sound options, particularly with an **apricot or pear** tart. Hungary's Tokaji 5 Puttonyos is good with **apple** tart, while German Eiswein, though extremely delicate in texture, has the sweetness to go well with **cherry** tart. A different kind of tart uses eggy **crème patissière** as the base, rather than frangipane, and is usually topped with glazed red fruits such as raspberries or strawberries. These are lighter in texture, and need suitably lighter wines, such as the late-picked Muscats and Rieslings of California or Australia. For the recently much sought-after **tarte Tatin**, a caramelised apple tart baked upside down, only an intensely sweet rotted wine will do. Roll out the Sauternes, or botrytised Semillons of Australia or South Africa. For **lemon tart**, see below.

Gâteaux Those show-stopping cakes that roll from table to table in the kinds of dining-rooms that still have dessert trolleys are usually heavily cemented with whipped cream and composed of layers of liqueur-soaked sponge, but despite that, are relatively light in texture. A **fruit** version such as orange or strawberry is best with light sweet Muscat, whether in the form of sparkling Asti or late-picked Alsace or Californian Muscat, while a very gooey **chocolate** gâteau will need a fortified Muscat, such as Muscat de Frontignan or Muscat de Beaumes-de-Venise. For that 1970s favourite **Black Forest Gâteau**, in which a light flavour of chocolate is mixed very appealingly with black cherry, try a glass of Californian Black Muscat, a light-textured, purple sweet wine with a beguiling hint of violet on the finish.

Gooseberry fool The tartness of this tartest of summer fruits, mulched into its sweetly creamy surround, calls for a sweet wine with balancing acidity, so reach for those botry-tised Loire wines – Coteaux du Layon or Quarts de Chaume. A Trockenbeerenauslese from Austria is another good bet.

Ice-creams and sorbets Opinions differ, but we are still not keen on the idea of drinking wine with frozen desserts, and for one very good reason: the coldness of the food partially numbs the tastebuds, preventing full appreciation of any accompanying wine. Furthermore, the more you eat, the more anaesthetised the tongue and palate become, so the problem only intensifies. In addition to that, there is something about the lightness of texture of ice-cream, and especially a water-based sorbet made without egg-white, that makes the introduction of alcohol on to the palate seem annoyingly crude and intrusive. If you really can't do without, the simplicity of something like Moscato d'Asti will just about do with fruit-flavoured ice-creams (its very low alcohol, around 5%, helps in this context), but the sparkling version is not so good, as the bubbles get in the way. As a way of short-circuiting the whole process, much enjoyment can be had from pouring a quantity of oozingly viscous PX sherry (made from raisined grapes), or its southern-hemisphere equivalent, one of the Liqueur Muscats of Rutherglen in the state of Victoria, Australia, over a bowl of vanilla ice-cream. You are arguably then turning the wine into an ingredient in the dish, which isn't quite the same thing as matching wine to food. If you find it irresistible, though, who cares?

Iles flottantes Soft-cooked whipped egg-white islands floating on a sea of vanilla crème anglaise, this French classic cries out for a botrytised wine to go with it. The smooth, caramelly quality of Sauternes, or one of its less expensive neighbours, such as Loupiac or Cadillac, are superb with it, and so, naturally, are their Californian and Australian counterparts, the noble-rotted Semillons.

Jam roly-poly A hot, suety roll filled with jam and served with custard, this is a dyed-in-the-wool British pudding with absolutely no pretensions to grandeur.

Drink a glass of chilled Moscatel de Valencia with it. This is a fortified sweet grape juice that hasn't undergone any fermentation. A similar product, perhaps a cut above it in fact, is Pineau des Charentes from the Cognac region of France. It too should be served well-chilled.

Lemon meringue pie The airiness of the beaten egg-white suggests a light sweet wine, and the tartness of the lemon one with sharply defined acidity. Go with a sweet Chenin Blanc from either South Africa or the Loire (Vouvray moelleux a good choice for the latter).

Lemon tart Sweet Chenin is as good with this custard-based lemon dessert as with lemon meringue pie (see above), but the richer filling and the buttery pastry need a richer version of the wine. Quarts de Chaume, Coteaux du Layon and Bonnezeaux from the central Loire Valley are all fantastic with lemon tart. German Beerenauslese wines made from Riesling, particularly from the Rheingau and Pfalz regions, also shine, and the odd English dessert wine, if sweet enough, is good too.

Mince pies As well as being the treat for churchgoers returning from Midnight Mass on Christmas Eve, mince pies make a popular festive dessert, warmed up and with cream poured over them. A glass of sweet Hungarian Tokaji does well as a partner to them, and so – at the other end of the spectrum – does a sweetish sparkler such as Moscato Spumante, or even the rare, sweeter style of champagne labelled Rich.

Mousses Fruit-flavoured mousses, set by means of beaten separated egg-white, are best eaten with a featherlight sweet wine such as a German Eiswein, Italian Moscato d'Asti, or one of the lighter Californian or Australian late-picked Muscats. For chocolate mousse, see the separate entry above.

Pancakes and maple syrup This all-American treat is naturally a very sweet dish that calls for a particularly

syrupy accompanying wine. Austrian and German Trockenbeerenauslese is the sort of thing to match it, but for a
more home-grown suggestion, a botrytised Riesling from
California will suit the mood admirably too.

Pavlovas These indulgent creations of meringue, fruit
and whipped cream are unexpectedly tricky to match with
wine. It's something to do with the sweet, brittle but
essentially flavourless quality of the meringue. Spain's
Moscatel de Valencia isn't bad, and for a fizzy suggestion,
a sweet Italian pink frizzante would do, especially if the
dish contains red fruit such as raspberries.

Pecan pie America's sticky-rich pecan pie needs a big,
toffeeish fortified wine to do it justice. Anything less will
be quite obliterated. The best two candidates are sweet
madeira (Bual or, even better, Malmsey) or a marsala
dolce from Sicily, but you might even profitably try a rich,
dark oloroso sherry.

Pithiviers A traditional French dessert that consists of
almond cream in a puff pastry base, a pithiviers is best
supported by a gentle botrytised wine such as a Sauternes
or Monbazillac, an Alsace Sélection de Grains Nobles
Pinot Gris, or – perhaps best of all – one of the sweetest
styles of Jurançon from southwest France.

Poached pear A poached pear doesn't obviously call out
for a wine to go with it, but a way can be found nonetheless. If the pear is cooked in a spicy **red wine syrup**, as is
traditional, with a sharpening note from citrus zests, one
of the unusual sweet fortified reds of southern France
works well – either Banyuls or Maury. A botrytised Riesling performs better if the pear is served in the **belle Hélène**
style, with chocolate sauce.

Profiteroles A favourite dessert of the 1970s, profiteroles
are balls of choux pastry filled with cream and served with
a rich chocolate sauce. Late-picked Muscats, Rieslings and
Gewürztraminers all chime in harmoniously in their

company, and sparkling Asti is once again a star.

Raspberries With a bowl of perfectly ripe, fresh raspberries, a fashionable accompaniment in recent years has been a glass of dry red wine. It sounds unlikely but genuinely does work. The best two grape varieties to go for are Gamay (as in Beaujolais) or Pinot Noir (as in burgundy). To chill the wine adds greatly to the pleasure of this combination, but it only really works if you hold off from the sugar and cream.

Rice pudding Trendy though it has become of late, rice pudding doesn't seem one of the most obvious dishes to drink wine alongside. Its bland, homogenous, milky texture seems to be quite enough on its own. That said, a small glass of something like Australia's Orange Muscat and Flora wouldn't go amiss, and neither would a tiny tot of decent pale cream sherry.

Rum baba This rum-soaked sponge filled with raisins is no great friend of wine, at least if it's made with rum, that is. A glass of Hungary's Tokaji 5 Puttonyos, or the even more opulent Tokaji Aszu, seems about the best strategy to cope with it. Variations on the baba use the cherry liqueur, kirsch, instead of rum, and it wouldn't exactly bring the temple of gastronomy crashing down were you to experiment with some of the fortified dessert wines in its place. That way, if you used, for example, one of Australia's powerful Rutherglen Liqueur Muscats in the recipe, you could happily drink some alongside it.

Sherry trifle The most obvious recourse might seem to be to partner the dish with a measure of whatever sweet sherry you have used in the recipe, but that can be a little overwhelming alongside the fruit and custard layers of the trifle. A fortified southern French Muscat, such as Beaumes-de-Venise, Frontignan or St-Jean-de-Minervois, is a much more sensitive partner.

Steamed sponge puddings Once the backbone of the

British pudding repertoire, steamed sponges, while they sound heavy, are actually quite light-textured on the palate. The choice, though, depends very much on the topping. Spanish Moscatel de Valencia is about the best choice with the intense sweetness of a **syrup or treacle** sponge, while Moscato d'Asti or sparkling Asti makes a refreshing partner for one topped with **jam**. Try the sweet variation on one of Italy's dry whites, Recioto di Soave, with a **ginger** sponge, while Muscat de Beaumes-de-Venise would be the best option for a **chocolate** sponge with its own sauce.

Strawberries and cream One of those summer dishes that exists, in some people's minds, for the sole purpose of ruining a bottle of champagne, strawberries are much happier with late-picked Muscats and Rieslings from Alsace, Germany, California, Australia or South Africa. If you come across it, a German product, Strawberry Wine Cup, which is a mixture of strawberry juice in sweet white wine, would be a very happy choice. You could even pour some of it into the dish.

Summer pudding The tart juices of summer berries that gush forth from this bread pudding pose a problem for most sweet wines. You could try a lightly chilled red, such as Brouilly from the Beaujolais region, but for a true dessert wine, probably the best option is to stick to sparkling Asti.

Syllabub If you have used a sweet wine in the recipe for this extremely simple, creamy, old English dessert, then it makes sense to drink a glass of whatever it was alongside it too. If you are eating it in a restaurant, or somebody else has made it, stick to the safest course, and go for a botrytised Semillon or Riesling from Australia, South Africa or California to match the creamy density of the dish.

Tiramisu An old Venetian recipe that shot to prominence in the 1980s, tiramisu is a softly squelchy mixture of eggs, mascarpone, coffee, cream and marsala. Not surprisingly, a small glass of sweet (dolce) marsala works beautifully with it, as does the slightly less powerful flavour of Italian vin santo. But the opulent dessert wines of Sauternes and Barsac are also unutterably delicious with it, and the grandness of the dish seems to merit them.

Toffee bananas The only dessert (apart from ice-cream or lychees) that Westerners are ever tempted to eat in a Chinese restaurant, toffee bananas may well have to rub along with whatever limited choice (if any) of sweet wine there is on the wine list. If you're recreating the dish at home, however, one of the sweet Muscats is by far the best option, whether it be Beaumes-de-Venise, Australian Orange Muscat and Flora, or even the light Orange Muscat of California.

Treacle tart Such an exceedingly sweet dessert will make all but the very sweetest wines taste strangely thin and sour. Some advocate Asti in the hope that the bubbles might just cut through all the sugar, but the truth is that the wine just isn't sweet enough. Fortified French Muscats do reasonably well, as does a small glass of Malmsey madeira, but the best match we have tried is the orange-scented syrupiness of Portugal's fortified Setúbal Moscatel.

Zabaglione Tougher than you might think to match, this Italian speciality consists of a warmly frothy mixture of sweet marsala, egg yolks and sugar, and is usually served in a wineglass. A tot of marsala dolce on the side seems somehow superfluous. Asti, for cutting the glutinous texture of it, would be a more appealing partner.

11

CHEESES

In those countries where there was no great tradition of drinking wine, and particularly in the UK, cheeses were the food with which many people first tentatively tried it out. The wine and cheese evening of blessed memory wasn't an unalloyed joy in the sense that it did involve stuffing oneself with rather more cheese than was quite seemly at one occasion, but the function it performed in introducing people to different styles of wine – and, even more importantly, to the principle of matching wine and food – was a valuable one.

Ever since then, we have felt, rightly enough, that the two commodities are natural partners, and so they are in countries where there is a historic winemaking culture. The French would barely think of setting about one of their cheeses without an accompanying glass of wine, and they have some very stimulating ideas about what goes with what. In the English-speaking countries, though, we tend to be somewhat less adventurous, sticking either to red wines or, more traditionally, to port when the cheeseboard sallies forth. 'Good with cheese', announces the back label on many a bottle of red wine, which only leaves one rather immense question hanging in the air: 'which cheese?'

There could hardly be a more elaborately diverse food

category than cheese. There are cheeses made from cow's, goat's, sheep's and even buffalo's milk, and new ones are being invented all the time. The range of textures available is as broad as the oceans, and the same cheese may come in various guises according to its level of maturity. With all this in mind, it hardly makes sense to try to match one wine to a selection of hugely different cheeses on a board. If you have been following our advice through all the succeeding stages of a dinner menu, now is the time above all to exercise restraint. There is nothing wrong – indeed it's become rather chic in recent years – with serving one prime specimen at the end of a meal. If you have a perfectly ripe cheese in good condition from a creamery or deli whose products you trust implicitly (the kind of place where they are happy to let you taste the cheese before deciding whether to buy some), then let it be the star of the final course. That way, you can put the same amount of thought into choosing an appropriate wine to go with it.

It may be that you don't want to open another whole bottle at this stage of the evening, when a fair few corks will likely have been drawn already. This is the logic, of course, in serving a tot of some fortified wine to round things off, but there is nothing to stop you having a single small glass of the accompanying wine, and recorking and saving the rest (see Chapter 1 for advice on such matters). Then again, a fine, ripe cheese and some good crusty bread, perhaps with some salad leaves on the side, can make an admirably sustaining lunch, and then a bottle of wine among two or three of you won't go amiss either.

The greatest revelation contained in the pages that follow, for those who haven't yet ventured further than port or claret with cheese, is that so many white wines perform so well with it. There are cheeses that are much happier with either dry or sweet white wines than with reds, and even though the back labels on the bottles never suggest as much, you will find a world of gustatory satisfaction awaiting you in these combinations.

We have elected in this chapter to divide the cheeses stylistically rather than by country of origin, since this is how most of us decide what types of cheeses we'd like to eat. In each case, we have assumed that the cheese you buy will be the ripest and fullest-flavoured example of its kind, in other words, that it will be in optimum condition, perfectly mature and yet fresh. Always remember to give cheese a period of time out of the fridge before serving it. If it's too cold, you're losing many of the subtleties in its flavour, which means you aren't getting your money's worth out of it. We're also assuming that, while you may want a hunk of bread or a plain biscuit or two with your cheese, you might be prepared to dispense with the full panoply of celery, grapes and so on that often comes with a cheese platter. Most importantly of all, be aware that the flavours of most sweet or sour chutneys and relishes will mutilate the flavour of wine. Avoid.

GOAT'S-MILK CHEESES
Unlike sheep's-milk cheeses, there is basically only one universal style of goat's cheese generally available. The French know it as chèvre, but there are also some very good UK versions, with the Welsh product having the distinct edge over the English. It typically has a chalky, dry texture, and can be very light in flavour if too young, but a properly mature example will have the telltale goaty pungency that makes it such a good salad ingredient. Served fresh on its own, as opposed to being melted over something as a starter (for which, see Chapter 4), goat's cheese is best with crisp, dry white wines with a fair amount of juicy fruit. Sauvignon Blanc is an absolute winner with it, especially the opulent Sauvignons of the upper Loire

(Pouilly-Fumé, Sancerre, Menetou-Salon, Quincy and Reuilly), the very area where one of the best French goat's cheeses of them all, Crottin de Chavignol, is made. The less illustrious Touraine Sauvignon of the central Loire is fine too. South Africa's Sauvignons are superb in this context, and the New Zealand wines of the Marlborough region are close behind them. At a comparable price to the Touraine wines, Sauvignons from Hungary should by no means be overlooked. Otherwise, Riesling makes a good match, as long as the wine is properly dry (think Alsace, Australia or New Zealand), and even the dry Chenin wines of the Loire, such as Vouvray sec, work well.

SHEEP'S-MILK CHEESES

These come in many different forms, southern Europe being an especially rich source of all sorts of obscure examples, which are not generally seen outside their countries of origin, but which are always worth trying when you come across them. The quartet listed here are the four internationally known types.

Feta A name that has become almost as abused as that of Cheddar, real feta should be made exclusively from sheep's milk (many are a blend of sheep's and goat's), and should ideally come from either Greece or Cyprus – not France, not Denmark, not anywhere else. Feta is matured in brine, making it an exceptionally salty, sharp-flavoured cheese, and while it tends to be more useful as a salad ingredient, it can also be very satisfying to eat on its own. It's a white wine cheese, and the same kinds of dry Sauvignon and Riesling that go with goat's cheese (see above) will perform well here too. High acidity in the wine is a positive boon. Spanish and Italian whites will come to no harm, provided they are crisp enough (Rias Baixas and Frascati Superiore, respectively, would be good choices), and the proper cultural match is of course with one of the new wave of Greek white wines. Retsina, the only Greek white wine that most people have heard of, is a traditional, but not particularly good, partner. The pronounced muskiness in the wine, gained from its being matured with lumps of pine resin in it, tends to predominate.

Manchego Spain's most famous sheep's cheese is a hard-textured, and very appetising, premium product. The older versions have as much concentrated, savoury flavour as mature Parmesan, and the cheese is often sold in slices immersed in olive oil. It has a salty, firm but crumbly texture in the mouth. Red wines with some cask-ageing but a distinct element of freshening acidity in them are the best matches with this cheese. The local red is Valdepeñas, made in the south of La Mancha, and it works reasonably well, although some older versions might lack the stuffing to cope with a mature cheese. Rioja Crianza or Reserva, from further north, is a surer bet, and even the sturdy textures of Ribera del Duero red don't overwhelm good Manchego. Wandering further afield, Portuguese reds from the Douro and Alentejo regions are excellent, as are some of the sharper reds of Italy, Barbera d'Alba and Chianti Rufina foremost among them. Outside Europe, the Spanish and Italian varietals of Argentina, California and Australia are the wines to seek out: Tempranillo, Sangiovese, Bonarda and Nebbiolo.

Pecorino This is the generic name given to sheep's cheeses from various regions of Italy, deriving from the Italian word for sheep, *pecora*. The styles vary quite widely, but probably the best-known outside Italy is Pecorino Romano, which looks very white, and has a hard, crumbly, salty texture that enables it to be used as a cheese for grating over a hot dish (it's a sharper alternative to Parmesan for grating over risotto). On its own, it's perhaps better with a dry white than with a red, and pungent Loire or South African Sauvignons suit it to a T. A good, mature Muscadet de Sèvre-et-Maine *sur lie* would make a particularly appetising match with ripe Pecorino.

Roquefort France's most famous sheep's cheese is a blue variety, and is listed below under blue cheeses.

BUFFALO-MILK CHEESE

Mozzarella Although much of it these days is made from cow's milk, the original mozzarella is made from the milk of the European water buffalo. It is a very soft, pasty, snow-white cheese with a tantalisingly mild flavour. Mostly used on pizza toppings, it can also be eaten on its own, or classically in a simple salad, accompanied by big slices of beef tomato and leaves of fresh basil. Its delicacy of flavour is such that only the lightest dry whites will sit well with it. Italian whites such as Gavi, Vernaccia di San Gimignano, Albana di Romagna and Soave Classico are all it needs. South African Colombard shouldn't startle it, and nor should Alsace Pinot Blanc, but avoid the fruitier varieties such as Sauvignon or Riesling.

SOFT COW'S-MILK CHEESES

Some of the world's very greatest cheeses are these soft to semi-soft cow's-milk products, but their yielding, often positively runny, texture makes it quite difficult to find a precise balance with wine. Most of those listed here are from France, but there are also examples from Italy, Switzerland, Ireland and Wales.

Bel Paese Made in Lombardy, Bel Paese is sold in foil-wrapped portions and is very good for spreading on thin biscuits. Its buttery flavour and softly pasty texture make it better with white wines than reds. Stick to its country of origin, and choose an Italian white such as Soave, Verdicchio or Gavi to accompany it, or else one of the unoaked Chardonnays of the Alto Adige region. Reds are mostly too heavy for it, but a light Sangiovese di Romagna, or something like a Ciro or Squinzano from further south should oblige.

Boursin This French cheese comes with admixtures of garlic and herbs or crushed peppercorns (for which see later, under Value-Added Cheeses), but there is a plain version too. It tends to be fairly creamy but bland, and is brought out of itself by being matched with crisp, herbaceous, fruity whites, Loire Sauvignons and Alsace Riesling to the fore. With reds, it suffers a little, but the gentlest style of Burgundian Pinot Noir shouldn't upset it too much.

Brie The designation Brie covers a multitude of sins, mostly in the shape of immature cheeses that are much too firm in texture. Good French Brie should be soft and yielding (but not oozingly runny), with a clean white rind and shiny centre. It is very good with light rustic French reds, such as Gamay de Touraine, and some of the red wines of the Loire Valley: Chinon, Saumur-Champigny and St-Nicolas-de-Bourgueil. Light Pinot Noirs from New Zealand or California can work well with it. Whites with a certain amount of grassy pungency, particularly if the cheese itself is unpasteurised, are a good fit too. Look to South African and Hungarian Sauvignon Blanc or Australian Colombard. Mature Chablis can be a good match, but a lightly flavoured, young wine will be overwhelmed by the cheese.

Camembert Much the same applies to Camembert as to Brie. It is sold through supermarkets in much too young a state. Go to a good deli for a more mature, pungently aromatic cheese that has a real waft of the barnyard about it. The same kinds of wines as go with Brie are good with Camembert as well, except that the reds can afford to be a little more intense. Mature burgundy, such as Gevrey-Chambertin or Nuits St-Georges, is decadently enjoyable with it, and an older vintage of Morgon or Moulin-à-Vent from Beaujolais is almost equally good. Lightly oaky Chardonnay turns out to be a fine match, as long as it has a decent balancing note of acidity. The pays d'Oc, Chile and New Zealand are good areas to look.

Chaource A creamy northern French cheese of ancient lineage, made near Troyes, Chaource is happiest with a crisp white wine, such as dry Vouvray, Touraine Sauvignon or one of the lesser-known whites of Cheverny or Haut-Poitou. A mature Muscadet de Sèvre-et-Maine *sur lie* also suits it. Outside Europe, choose a high-acid, but fairly plain white, such as unoaked Chardonnay from the Casablanca region of Chile, coastal South Africa or Tasmania.

Chaumes Orange-rinded Chaumes is a semi-soft cheese with a fairly bland, lightly buttery flavour. It's best with lightly creamy whites without too much pronounced fruit, such as Pinot Blanc from Alsace, northern Italian Chardonnays from Trentino and Alto Adige, Spanish whites from the Parellada, Macabeo and Chardonnay varieties, and simple southern-hemisphere blends of Colombard and Chardonnay.

Epoisses One of the greatest of all soft cheeses, Epoisses deserves to be much better-known than it is. Among the speciality cheeses in the supermarket, it is often a better bet for strong, rounded, rustic flavour than the Brie or Camembert on offer. Its yellowy-brown rind is washed in either white wine or some wine distillate or eau-de-vie. One of the best types, Chambertin, is washed in marc de Bourgogne, the grape spirit made from the pressed skins left over after winemaking. Since it's a Burgundian cheese, it seems obvious to start there, and you will find a mature, cask-fermented white wine of more use than a red. The most opulent whites – Meursault, Puligny-Montrachet, even Corton-Charlemagne – are heavenly with a piece of ripe Epoisses, but the lesser wines will work perfectly well too. Oaky Chardonnays from California, Chile, South Africa and New Zealand are in the next rank. Pinot Noir reds can work, provided that they are not too tannic; soft cheeses hate tannin. Go for a Beaune or Pommard, or one of the softer Pinots of California's Carneros region, as long as it has at least three years' bottle-age.

Livarot Profoundly pungent from being matured in unventilated sheds, Livarot is a Normandy cheese with a long and distinguished history. Like Epoisses, it needs a big, assertive wine to carry it. Mature, high-alcohol Chardonnay can work, as long as it isn't full of tropical fruit flavours. Some of the wines of Chile, Washington State or Oregon are good in this regard, as are big eastern Spanish whites with Chardonnay in the blend. In France itself, the vin de pays d'Oc Chardonnays can be fine, as can some of the heavier whites of the Rhône, such as St-Joseph or Châteauneuf-du-Pape blanc. Mature, farmyardy red burgundy also comes into its own once again.

Maroilles Originally a monastic cheese dating back to the tenth century, Maroilles has an orange rind and softish centre, but doesn't have quite the pungency of flavour that Epoisses or Livarot can lay claim to. A delicate red, such as Gamay de Touraine, isn't bad with it, but it is much happier with white wine of fairly neutral flavour. Vouvray sec, Côtes du Rhône blanc and Alsace Pinot Blanc all fit the bill, and an unexpectedly good match can be found with blanc de blancs champagne. By the same token, light sparklers made by the traditional method from California or New Zealand, as well as some of the better-made Spanish cavas, make successful partners.

Mascarpone This delicious soft Italian cheese with its featherlight, whipped-cream consistency is not much eaten on its own. It tends to be served in Italy with fruit, or with its flavour slightly modified in some way, such as with sweet spice. We know it better as a dessert ingredient in such indulgences as tiramisu. Try serving it, though, with chopped dried apricot as a post-pudding treat, and partner it with a small glass of Muscat de Beaumes-de-Venise, or a decent ripe Italian Vin Santo.

Milleens Perhaps the very greatest of the modern generation of Irish cheeses, Milleens is made in the west of County Cork, and is a tangy, pungently rustic soft cheese with enough personality to give a mature Livarot a run for its money. A light, surprisingly basic red is rather good with it – something like Côtes du Rhône-Villages or one of the Languedoc reds such as Minervois or St-Chinian. Mature burgundy is a star once again, though, as with Epoisses; whites with a fair amount of oaky richness are good too (try a white Rioja Crianza or dry white Bordeaux from Pessac-Léognan).

Munster Cheese doesn't get much more strongly flavoured than this Alsace specimen. Even in France, they'll look askance at you if you get on public transport with some of it in your shopping. It has been made in the region since the seventh century, and goes with some – though not all – of the wines of Alsace. Riesling, Sylvaner and Pinot Blanc all make appetising matches, though Gewürztraminer and a lot of Pinot Gris tend to be too flowery and Muscat too citrussy. Reds are better though, with Grenache-Syrah blends coming out on top. Châteauneuf-du-Pape, Gigondas, Lirac and Vacqueyras are all excellent with it, as are the corresponding blends from Spain (Rioja and Navarra reds especially), Australia and California. The rarely seen Pinot Noirs of Alsace can be good, though most are way too light for the predominating flavour of the cheese.

Pencarreg A golden-yellow, glossy-centred cheese not dissimilar to good Brie, Pencarreg is made in Wales. Its flavour is strong, with a hint of fruitiness, and it works best with aromatic white wines such as Alsace Gewürztraminer and Pinot Gris, Gewürztraminers from Chile, South Africa and New Zealand, and Viogniers from Chile, California and the south of France. Reds mostly tend to clash with it.

Pont l'Evêque This Normandy cheese with its ridged, orangey rind and softish centre has a fresh, creamy flavour and forthright, though not overpoweringly strong, aroma. Light reds and grassy whites are its best friends. For the former, choose a Gamay (Brouilly, Fleurie or Chénas from Beaujolais), Pinot Noir, Italian Barbera or Sangiovese, or Italian varietals from Argentina. Among the latter, Sauvignons and Chenins are the safest bets, with the Loire, South Africa or New Zealand the places to look.

Port-Salut Not as strongly flavoured as many other soft cheeses, Port-Salut is a creamy-textured, washed-rind cheese made in the district of Lorraine. Mild whites are best with it, so think along the lines of Alsace Pinot Blanc, white Côtes du Rhône, Chablis and Bordeaux's Entre-deux-Mers, or go for a Colombard-Chardonnay blend from Australia or South Africa.

Reblochon Made in the Haute-Savoie region of eastern France, Reblochon is justifiably considered one of that country's very best cheeses. It has a semi-soft, richly creamy character, with a lightly moulded rind, and is usually sold between two discs of thin wood. Its rounded, full flavour makes it a winner with one of France's little-known speciality wines, the *vin jaune* of the Jura, produced not a million miles from where Reblochon itself is made. *Vin jaune* has a thick, sherry-like pungency, and if you can't find it, an aged (*viejo*) fino sherry could be just as good. Otherwise, stick to the richness of mature white burgundy or *premier cru* Chablis, or cask-fermented Chardonnays from California, Chile or South Africa – expensive wines, but this is one cheese that merits the outlay.

St-Marcellin A mildly flavoured, softly buttery cheese, St-Marcellin is rather overwhelmed by even the lightest reds, and is best with the kinds of dry whites suggested for Port-Salut.

Taleggio Occasionally one comes across a matured version of Taleggio, but essentially this is a gently flavoured, semi-soft, slightly nutty Italian cheese. Pair it with Soave Classico Superiore or Vernaccia di San Gimignano for the best matches, but simple unoaked Chardonnays from almost anywhere will do quite as well.

Vacherin Mont d'Or Versions of Vacherin are produced in eastern France, but this, undoubtedly the best type, is made over the border in Switzerland. At its best when it is gently runny, it has a luxuriously rich, creamy flavour, and is traditionally eaten from its wooden box with a spoon, after the top of the tan-coloured, wrinkly rind has been carefully removed. Not surprisingly, it works well enough with Switzerland's own delicate white wines, from such grape varieties as Fendant, Amigne and Savagnin. If you can't get hold of one of those (and they are eye-wateringly expensive if you do), try your luck with a Pinot Gris or Pinot Blanc from Alsace, a white Rhône such as Châteauneuf-du-Pape blanc, a Portuguese white such as Fernão Pires, or creamy but unoaked Chardonnays from Australia, Chile, South Africa or the United States.

HARD COW'S-MILK CHEESES
These are the easiest of all cheeses to find vinous partners for. They are, by and large, better suited to reds than to whites, but not exclusively so, as the following notes reveal.

Appenzell A fine Swiss cheese with a full, rounded flavour, Appenzell has a thick, deeply coloured rind that is washed in white wine. There is a distinct suggestion of spiciness on the aftertaste, which helps it to marry with spicy red wines, such as northern Rhône Syrah (try Crozes-Hermitage), or one of northern Italy's reds, such as Barbera or even the gentler versions of Barolo. Otherwise, choose a Shiraz or Shiraz-Cabernet from Australia, or a Syrah from California or Chile.

Beaufort A much underrated hard cheese from the Savoie region of France, Beaufort has a deep yellow paste and a texture very similar to that of mature Cheddar. The flavour is rich and buttery, invitingly smooth, and tastes wonderful with soft-textured Cabernet Sauvignon reds. Buy a Reserva from Chile, or one of South Africa's recent offerings. Gentle clarets from Pomerol and St-Emilion work majestically, as do the humbler Cabernets and Cabernet-Merlot blends of eastern Europe.

Caerphilly A traditional old Welsh cheese with a crumbly texture, generally made for eating young, although there is a heartening recent tendency to age it a little longer, Caerphilly is good with midweight rounded reds such as Californian Merlot, Australian Cabernet Sauvignon, Châteauneuf-du-Pape and Rioja Crianza, as well as with crisp, herbaceous whites like Sancerre and Alsace Riesling.

Cantal A densely textured, richly flavoured cheese that can trace its lineage back to Roman times, France's Cantal requires a mature red to do it justice. A claret from one of the lighter vintages will work well, as will the meatier styles of Beaujolais, such as Moulin-à-Vent. Spanish Tempranillo-based reds, Italian Barbera and Teroldego Rotaliano and Portugal's modern Douro Valley reds are great, as is the softly contoured style of Australian, Californian and Chilean Merlot.

Cheddar Much imitated (and traduced) around the world, true Cheddar comes only from the county of Somerset in the west of England. It also comes in a variety of strengths, from apologetically mild all the way up to the fully matured versions, which may have been kept for up to 18 months or so before release. Always look for the word 'farmhouse' on the label. They really are the best Cheddars. Reds are probably favourite, with mature Bordeaux from the Haut-Médoc or Pomerol districts a classic partner. Chianti Classico is a lovely match too, the acidity of the wine cutting the densely textured, buttery flavour of the cheese. Rioja Reserva performs well, and so do the soft-textured Merlots of California, Chile, Washington State and Australia. A tot of LBV (late-bottled vintage) port is another very traditional, successful match: the balance of sweet and savoury flavours is rich and satisfying. We also have to report that the outstanding match at one tasting of wines with Cheddar that we attended some years ago was with oaky Australian Chardonnay. The two types of butteriness worked exceptionally well together. It has to be tried to be believed. With **smoked Applewood Cheddar**, the combination is even better, because the smokiness imparted by the charred oak barrels the wine matures in matches the alluring flavour of the smoky cheese to perfection. Not only Australian Chardonnays, but those from Chile, California, New Zealand, South Africa and Burgundy are all superb.

Cheshire The crumbliness of Cheshire calls for a relatively delicate wine, although older farmhouse cheeses can have a more homogenous texture. A red with noticeable acidity, such as Cabernet Franc from the Loire (Bourgueil or Chinon), a young Beaujolais-Villages, or a New Zealand or Oregon Pinot Noir, is fine, and the gentler style of Sauvignon Blanc from California makes a suitable white partner. A mature Cheshire makes a very pleasant match with the lightest style of madeira, Sercial.

Comté Another French cheese of ancient lineage, Comté (named after the region of Franche-Comté) has a concentrated, nutty flavour. Rounded reds are the style of wine to seek out: Merlots from Chile and Washington State, Californian Zinfandel, Corbières or St-Chinian from the Languedoc.

Derby A fairly bland English cheese that is generally sold young, Derby can be eaten with a soft, everyday red such as Côtes du Rhône-Villages, or a straightforward unoaked Chardonnay from northern Italy, southern France or South Australia.

Double Gloucester A deeply coloured and creamy-textured cheese, this is crying out for a red wine to go with it. Gentle eastern European Cabernets, Californian Merlot, and the riper versions of South Africa's Pinotage are all fine. The southern Italian red Salice Salentino seems to match its texture exactly.

Edam The very shy flavour of red-rinded Dutch Edam would be quite overwhelmed by anything other than a fairly neutral, low-acid white. Italy's whites – Soave, Bianco di Custoza, Albana di Romagna, Vernaccia di San Gimignano, Gavi – are about all it can bear.

Emmenthal Swiss Emmenthal, with its firmish, holey texture, is a slightly slippery customer when it comes to wine. Most reds seem too tannic, and many whites appear to clash with it. Light northern Italian reds such as Teroldego Rotaliano and Merlot from the Veneto sit quietly alongside it, and a not-too-old Spanish Valdepeñas seems about right.

Fontina Delicately textured for a hard cheese, with a nutty, sweet-tasting paste, Fontina comes from the Valle d'Aosta in northwest Italy. Light reds don't do too badly with it (Barbera d'Alba is a good bet), but it is probably better with white wines that retain a touch of residual sweetness. Kabinett and Spätlese Rieslings from Germany's Mosel region work well, and so do the higher-alcohol Pinot Gris and Muscat of Alsace.

Gouda Firm and dry-textured, Dutch Gouda is definitely a red-wine cheese. The acerbic style of South Africa's Pinotage suits it, and so do the Italian varietals Sangiovese and Bonarda, as made in California or Argentina. Crozes-Hermitage from the northern Rhône isn't bad, and the velvety textures of cask-aged Rioja and Navarra reds are just right too.

Grana Padano This cheese is virtually indistinguishable to most palates – Italian ones included – from Parmesan, and so we refer you to the notes on that more famous cheese below.

Gruyère Proper Swiss Gruyère is an incomparable cheese, medium-firm with a springy texture and a sweet, moreishly nutty flavour. It is of course a great ingredient for cheese sauces, soufflés and gratins, but it makes a fine cheese course on its own too. It will sit happily alongside either reds or whites, although it probably prefers the latter. Dryish reds such as Médoc Bordeaux, Californian and Chilean Syrah, Chianti Classico and Rosso di Montalcino, and Garnacha-based Spanish reds are all good. In the white corner, Alsace Pinot Gris and Muscat, Vouvray demi-sec, Germany's and Austria's Kabinett Rieslings, and the lightly oaked Chardonnays of Australia are all stunningly successful.

Jarlsberg The only Norwegian cheese in this chapter, Jarlsberg had a brief flurry of popularity in the 1980s in the UK (Americans have always rated it), but it deserves to be consistently better known for its mild, sweetish flavour and creamy texture. Ripe white wines with juicy fruit flavours make the best matches. Go for Australian and New Zealand Rieslings and New Zealand Sauvignons.

Lancashire At its best one of England's very best cheeses, good Lancashire should be very pale, with a fine, grainy, crumbling texture and a sharp, acidic, refreshing flavour. Its flavour is best complemented by white wines that match its tang. Mature (i.e. at least three-year-old) Muscadet de Sèvre-et-Maine *sur lie* works well, as do those classic Sauvignons of the upper Loire, Sancerre and Pouilly-Fumé. Spain's Rueda is a success, and so is the austere style of Alsace Riesling. Young, vivacious, non-vintage champagne is a particularly fine match.

Leicester Known commercially as Red Leicester, as though there were any other colour, this is a mildly flavoured, firm cheese famous for its deep russet colour. A light white may do it justice (try Alsace Pinot Blanc), but it's really more content with softer reds such as Beaujolais, Italy's Dolcetto, or the lighter Merlots of Chile and central Europe.

Parmesan Always look for the words 'Parmigiano Reggiano' on the label to make sure you are getting the right thing. Italy's most famous cheese is used extensively for grating and shaving over pasta dishes and risottos, but a properly matured example (say, up to two years old) makes a fine cheese to eat on its own. Its flavour is a marriage of saltiness, sweetness and that slight hotness that mature hard cheeses impart to the palate, and it is surprisingly difficult to find a precise wine match. Many full, rounded reds such as southern-hemisphere Cabernet Sauvignons go all thin and mean and sour in its presence, but paradoxically the leaner, tarter flavours of many Italian reds work well. Salice Salentino from Puglia is a very obliging companion to it, Aglianico del Vulture is good, and so are the fuller reds of central Italy, such as Copertino and Montepulciano d'Abruzzo. Outside Italy, there are good matches with the sweetly oaky style of red Rioja Gran Reserva, some Languedoc and Roussillon reds such as Faugères or Collioures, and with the south-ern French fortified reds of Banyuls. A handful of gently oaky dry whites are successful too, beginning with the demi-sec (*abboccato*) style of Orvieto Classico, and going on through Alsace Pinot Gris, white Rioja Crianza, and lightly oaked Australian Chardonnays.

Provolone Once a rather sharp-tasting, pungent cheese, most Provolone is now sold younger, and has a delicate, mildly creamy flavour. Once again, the best matches are with its compatriot Italian wines, but with the gentler styles of Barbera d'Alba or Chianti Classico. Italian whites such as Lugana, Gavi and Arneis also work reasonably well with milder specimens.

Raclette A semi-hard Swiss cheese that is traditionally served in a melted state with piquantly flavoured accompaniments, Raclette can also be eaten just as it is, for its fully rounded, honeyed flavour. Swiss wines might be a bit too delicate for it, even the reds, but it makes an acceptable match with northern Rhône reds such as Crozes-Hermitage, or Syrah varietals from California or Chile.

St-Nectaire Another of France's historic cheeses, this one from the Auvergne, St-Nectaire has a richly buttery, though also quite mellow flavour. It's good with gently contoured reds such as cru Beaujolais (e.g. Juliénas or Fleurie) or Californian Gamay, with Côtes du Rhône-Villages, Spanish blends of Garnacha and Tempranillo (pre-eminently Rioja Crianza), and soft Merlots from eastern Europe, Chile or Washington State.

Tomme de Savoie/Tomme d'Abondance These semi-hard cheeses are made in eastern France, and have a deeply coloured paste, a slightly farmyardy aroma, and a savoury, nutty flavour. They need robust reds to accompany them: Châteauneuf-du-Pape, Vacqueyras, or a firmly textured Bordeaux from the Haut-Médoc or Graves. Syrah from California, Australian Shiraz-Cabernet blends and South Africa's Pinotage are also successful choices.

Wensleydale This white, crumbly, Yorkshire cheese is sold young, as ageing doesn't do a great deal for it. It has a mellow flavour, a little like Lancashire without quite the same bite. A demi-sec champagne is a very appetising match with it, as are light, crisp whites without too much predominant fruit flavour. Rieslings with a little residual sugar to them, such as Kabinett and Spätlese wines from Germany or Austria, go well. Reds are best avoided.

Yarg A modern classic, Cornish Yarg from southwest England is a mellow creamy cheese wrapped in nettles, which give it a gently herbaceous flavour. Its very best partner is with Loire Sauvignon Blanc – Sancerre, Pouilly-Fumé or Menetou-Salon – but it also works well with New Zealand Sauvignons, Alsace Rieslings and Spanish Verdejo. A red to accompany it would have to be fairly gentle: some of the softer styles of Languedoc red, such as Corbières or Minervois with at least a couple of years' bottle-age, would suffice.

BLUE CHEESES

Cheeses that have been allowed to mould under controlled conditions are among the greatest taste sensations in the world, and where once they were decidedly an acquired taste, they have now justly found widespread favour, with new varieties being created all the time. Don't think of them as all pretty much of a muchness, however: there is a huge spectrum of styles and strengths in those listed below.

Beenleigh Blue An English sheep's-milk blue made in Devon, Beenleigh has something of the yielding texture of Roquefort without that cheese's pronounced saltiness. A late-picked Muscat or Riesling from California or Australia makes a fine match with it, or try a Riesling Auslese or Beerenauslese from the Rheingau or Pfalz regions of Germany.

Bleu d'Auvergne Made in the mountains of the Massif Central, this pale, creamy, cow's-milk blue has relatively delicate-tasting paste, but the blue veining in it adds a strongly pungent note. Match it with a delicate wine and it will trample all over it. Sweet whites of any class tend to get stripped too, but a tot of well-chilled Moscatel de Valencia isn't too bad. Unexpectedly, a light, low-tannin red can work. Try a Brouilly or Beaujolais-Villages.

Bleu de Bresse A gentle-tasting cow's-milk blue originally conceived in imitation of Italy's Gorgonzola, Bresse matches happily with simple, sweet whites such as Auslese Rieslings from Germany or Austria, or else light reds such as the Gamays of Beaujolais or California, Italy's Dolcetto, or Italian Pinot Nero.

Blue Brie The blue version of Brie, mostly made in Germany (Cambozola is the best-known brand name), is best eaten with much the same wines as Bleu de Bresse (see above).

Blue Vinney Originally a Dorset cheese, but now mostly made in Leicestershire, this is a firm-textured, gently flavoured, cow's-milk blue with a passing resemblance to a milder Stilton. Gentle reds with low tannin work well with it, as in simple Côte de Beaune burgundy, Gamay de Touraine, Chinon from the Loire, and any of the lighter Pinot Noirs from outside Europe (Oregon's are a good bet).

Cashel Blue Ireland's pre-eminent blue is this luxuriously creamy, cow's-milk cheese made in County Tipperary. Its enveloping texture makes it hard to find a wine that precisely suits it, but the sweetly ripe character of Australian Cabernet Sauvignon isn't bad. Chilean Reserve Merlots perform reasonably well, but attempts to match the cheese with one of the sweet whites come to grief.

Danish Blue Invented about a century ago as an explicit alternative to Roquefort, Danish Blue – or Danablu to give it its native name – is an exceedingly strong-tasting, creamy, cow's-milk cheese with an almost metallic finish, which lingers on the palate for ages. We have yet to find a wine that doesn't suffer alongside it, but vigorously chilled fortified Muscats (e.g. Muscat de Rivesaltes) can counteract some of the saltiness of the cheese, while surrendering all their subtleties in the process.

Dolcelatte This putty-soft, starkly white, Italian cow's-milk cheese often has only the faintest hint of blueing, but the flavour is nonetheless quite strong. Soft reds, such as Teroldego Rotaliano, Pinot Nero, Dolcetto and Veneto Merlot from Italy, all work quite well, and an interesting contrast of flavours is set up with Moscato d'Asti.

Dunsyre Blue Made by the same producer as Lanark Blue (see below), this Scottish cheese is the cow's-milk counterpart to Lanark's sheep. The dense texture and pungent penicillin flavour demand a strongly constituted wine. LBV port copes with it, as do the tawny versions of port and medium-sweet amontillado sherry. Soft-centred reds aren't bad either: think Washington Merlot, Oregon Pinot, or Australian Cabernet Sauvignon.

Gorgonzola Italy's best blue is a richly creamy cheese, semi-soft when young, becoming firmer and slightly gritty as it ages, and with a lingering saltiness on the finish. It can be matched with gentle reds such as Italy's Barbera and Argentina's Bonarda, but is undoubtedly happier with sweet whites with a touch of noble rot, such as Monbazillac or Loupiac from France, Austrian Beerenauslese or a Quarts de Chaume from the Loire. Italy's own Vin Santo can be good, but the wine needs to be properly ripe and sweet to make a fitting marriage.

Lanark Blue Scotland's answer to Roquefort (made by the same producer as Dunsyre Blue, see above), Lanark is a decadently creamy sheep's-milk blue with mouth-filling pungency and a finish to beat the band. It needs a big rich dessert wine to do it justice, nothing less than cask-aged Sauternes or Barsac, or the equivalent botrytised Semillons of Australia, California or South Africa.

Roquefort For many the greatest blue cheese in the world, Roquefort is blued in caves at Combalou in the southwest of France. Made from sheep's milk, it has a milk-white paste with deep greenish-blue veining, and a high-octane flavour combining rich creaminess, penicillin pungency and emphatic saltiness. For its marriage made in heaven, it only needs to be introduced to the best rotted dessert wine you can afford. Botrytised Semillons, Rieslings and Chenins from all over the known world will go beautifully with it, but its classic partner is, without a doubt, classed-growth Sauternes or Barsac from Bordeaux.

St-Agur A modern cow's-milk blue made in the Auvergne, St-Agur is a mildly salty and gently flavoured cheese best partnered with the kinds of gentle reds that are recommended with Bleu de Bresse (see above).

Stilton One of England's great cheeses, and traditionally afforded rather more legal protection than Cheddar ever has been, blue Stilton is a densely textured cow's-milk cheese with a deep yellow paste, a rough, stubbly rind and a long, mellow but powerful, blue-mould flavour. Its time-honoured Christmas tablemate is red port, a mature vintage if the budget permits. We are a house divided as to the merits of this combination, with one of us not keen on it at all. Aged tawny port (go for a 10-year-old) is a much better bet, and the richer styles of madeira (Malmsey and Bual) are fabulous. Sweet whites, though, are definitely not happy with Stilton. Rounded, mellow reds, on the other hand, such as Californian Zinfandel, Cabernet Sauvignon from Australia's Coonawarra region, and Chile's and New Zealand's Merlots all work well.

VALUE-ADDED CHEESES
These are never our first choices from the cheeseboard, but they are a proliferating category of cheeses, and some of

them aren't bad. Additives can range from garlic, herbs and spices, through pieces of fruit, to chopped smoked meats and even ginger.

By and large, they are better with dry white wines than anything else. The **garlic and herb** version of Boursin is good with Sauvignon Blanc from Touraine, South Africa, Hungary or Australia, while the **peppercorn** version is fine with a southern French or Chilean Viognier, but will also go with a Rhône Syrah or Australian Shiraz.

Light English cheeses with **fruit pieces** (such as apricot or cranberry) are good with fruity whites like New Zealand Sauvignon, Chilean Chardonnay or German Rieslings of the Kabinett or Spätlese class.

Brown-rinded Bavarian smoked cheese with bits of **ham** in it is a red wine cheese, though not a particularly illustrious product. Simple southern Rhône, Californian and Australian red blends of Syrah/Shiraz and Grenache are fine with it.

A Scottish version of Cheddar flavoured with Isle of Arran **mustard** is a surefire match for a richly smoky Chardonnay that has been aged in barrel, with Burgundy, California and Chile leading the charge.

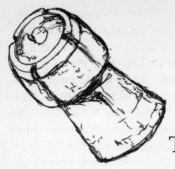

12

THE *RIGHT FOOD* WITH THE RIGHT WINE

Sooner or later, if you're anything like us, you will find yourself overcome by the impulse to plan a dinner around a bottle or two of wine, rather than the other way around. This is quite as legitimate an approach gastronomically, and just as much fun. Supposing that favourite uncle has gifted you a bottle of ostentatious claret on some landmark birthday, or you have won a magnum of something fizzy at the church fête, or else an exciting new wine, or fine vintage of a classic wine, has just caught your eye in the wine merchant's. Suddenly, you find it's burning a hole in the cellar, or the bottom of the wardrobe or wherever you've squirrelled it away, and you decide the time has come for it to see the light of day. What are you going to eat with it?

Naturally, this approach permits of just as much flexibility as matching the wine to the food does. In the listing below, we take a whirlwind tour of the world's principal wine styles and grape varieties, and attempt to give a potted series of suggestions for things you might like to eat with them, covering as many of the food categories in the earlier part of this book as are appropriate for each one.

This is by no means an exhaustive exercise, and we encourage you to make your own notes as you go along as to what works best with what, building up a databank of your own to supplement ours, and which will stand you in good stead in the future. After all, when a wine and food combination has proved truly remarkable, as they regularly do, why let the experience recede into the mists of memory? Make a record of it, so that when the time comes to enjoy a particular dish or wine again – either at home or eating out – you have a ready resource to point you in the direction of one of its best gastronomic companions.

SPARKLING WINES

Asti Asti (and its close cousin Moscato Spumante) are light, low-alcohol, sweetly frothy wines, perfect for the lightest desserts. Fruit-based mousses, light gâteaux, soufflés, profiteroles with chocolate sauce, and – perhaps most fitting of all – Christmas pudding and mince pies are the foods it's happiest with.

Australian sparkling reds The densely textured sparkling Cabernet Sauvignon and Shiraz reds that Australia has made a wine style all of its own are a little tricky to pair with food. They can be quite dry and tannic, in which case they can go reasonably well with barbecued meats, or as sweet as a drink of blackcurrant cordial, in which case we admit defeat and suggest that they are probably best drunk on their own.

Cava The flagship sparkling wine of Spain is still too hugely variable in quality to make blanket recommendations with food. When fresh and light and lemony (some in this style are labelled blanc de blancs, after the champagne terminology), they are excellent with Spanish tapas, cutting through the oiliness of the little appetisers, and even holding up reasonably well against the spicy sausage, chorizo. Too many, though, still taste stale and weary, which is pretty much how they will make you feel after drinking them.

Champagne Nowhere near as versatile with foods as many like to think, champagne is in fact as fussy as a maiden aunt when it comes to what company it's prepared to tolerate. Many foods make it seem thinner and sharper than it needs to be, while others simply stomp all over the subtleties of what is, even at its richest, a delicate style of wine. **Blanc de blancs**, the sort that's made entirely from Chardonnay, is a fine aperitif, as are most of the ordinary **non-vintage** (or NV) wines. NVs are also good with certain white, crumbly, English cheeses such as Lancashire and Wensleydale, and will rub along with the plainest fish dishes (fillets of white fish plainly grilled but not richly sauced). The lesser-known **blanc de noirs** (made exclusively from the black grapes, Pinot Noir and Pinot Meunier) can be a surprising hit with rich, creamy soups. **Demi-sec** champagnes are satisfying with a selection of nuts (walnuts, almonds, pistachios) at the end of a meal, but are mostly not sweet enough to accompany desserts. The sweetest styles of champagne, those labelled **Rich**, can be a treat with warm mince pies and cream as a pudding course. **Pink** (rosé) champagnes are reasonably good with seafood canapés, as long as there isn't too much mayonnaise about. If in doubt, drink champagne on its own as an appetite-whetter. This is its proudest role.

Other sparkling wines Sparkling wines of other regions, such as the Californian, Australian, New Zealand and South African sparklers that are made by the same method as champagne (look for the words 'Traditional Method' on the label), will serve in much the same categories as champagne itself. Many, though, tend to be a little sturdier and more full-bodied, an attribute that better equips them for drinking alongside food. Lightly dressed seafood salads, lightly sauced white fish dishes and something like poached chicken breast shouldn't overwhelm them.

WHITE WINES

Aligoté A little-known grape that appears as a bit-part player in the Burgundy region, Aligoté makes a lemon-sharp, rather acerbic style of dry white, occasionally leavened in the better ones (look for the village name Bouzeron on the label) with a delicate sour-cream softness. The typical acidity of the wine makes it a surefire candidate for accompanying shellfish dressed in mayonnaise, anything with garlic butter (mushrooms, prawns, snails), seafood salads or those containing avocado, and pâtés of oily smoked fish such as mackerel, salmon and trout.

Chardonnay The sky is (virtually) the limit with this most versatile of all white grape varieties. The **unoaked or lightly oaked** styles from the cooler climates (Chablis, southern Burgundy, northern Italy, coastal South Africa, New Zealand, Tasmania, Canada) are the most adaptable of all, happily partnering anything from highly seasoned canapés, most shellfish and fish dishes, lobster salad, lightly sauced and even roasted poultry, the lighter-textured game birds, sweetbreads, milder ethnic dishes such as Indian chicken dhansak or pad thai (Thailand's beansprouts and noodles), and even some of the lighter-textured hard cow's-milk cheeses. Richer wines that have been **fermented in oak**, or given an extended maturation time in barrels, need correspondingly richer dishes. They are excellent with smoked salmon and other smoked fish, cooked lobster and crab dishes, richly sauced poultry, roast guinea-fowl and pheasant, some of the creamier Indian chicken dishes (such as korma), and mature Somerset Cheddar.

Chenin Blanc The **driest** styles of Chenin, from the Loire or South Africa, are wines with assertively high acidity, and are just made for cold shellfish and crustacean dishes, plainly grilled white fish such as lemon sole, plaice and freshwater fish, and grilled smoked haddock. A glass of dry Chenin with onion bhajis works well, and it is a good background to the light spicing of king prawn biryani. **Off-dry** Chenin (e.g. Vouvray demi-sec) is better with creamier Indian dishes such as pasanda, Peking duck, most dim sum dishes, and gravad lax. The sweetest style of Vouvray, **moelleux**, is a dessert wine to go with eggy sweet dishes such as egg custard tart and lemon meringue pie. The **botrytised** styles of Chenin Blanc, of which the Loire wines Quarts de Chaume, Bonnezeaux and Coteaux du Layon are the torchbearers, are among the richest and most opulent of all dessert wines, but always retain a freshening element of lemony acidity to them. Drink them with lemon tart, apple pie, baked apple, gooseberry crumble, and fruit cheesecakes.

Colombard A fairly neutral grape variety often seen as a blending partner with Chardonnay in everyday dry whites of South Africa and Australia, Colombard is good when forthright spicing in a dish calls for a wine that won't suffer too much. Thai fishcakes with chilli sauce or wasabi-hot Japanese sushi are the kinds of foods to consider.

Gewürztraminer Its spiritual home may be Alsace, where it makes some of the most startlingly perfumed and richly concentrated white wines in the world, but good examples are now emerging from Chile, South Africa, New Zealand, central Europe and Washington State as well. **Dry** versions are excellent with many spicy cuisines, particularly those of Thailand and China, with smoked salmon and other smoked fish, creamy-sauced fish main courses (especially salmon), and certain soft cow's-milk cheeses, such as Pencarreg from Wales. **Late-picked** wines (e.g. Alsace Vendange Tardive) go well with hot fruit soufflés and fruit-flavoured bavarois, while the very sweetest **rotted** wines (Sélection de Grains Nobles in Alsace) are superb with crêpes suzette and cinnamon-flavoured apple pie.

Grüner Veltliner Austria's indigenous white speciality grape produces wines that are starkly dry and spicy, with plenty of alcohol and a peppery austerity to them. Drink it with the firmer-textured fish such as sea bass, or richly prepared fish such as paupiettes of sole stuffed with mushrooms, and with assertively spiced oriental dishes like sushi rolls, Chinese salt-and-pepper squid, and Thai red curries. Pork tenderloin served with mustard sauce won't faze it either.

Marsanne One of the grapes of the white wines of the northern Rhône has become something of a speciality in parts of South Australia, where it makes a ripe, tropical-fruited wine of considerable weight. It can be good with the meaty texture of fried John Dory, with China's black bean sauce dishes made with chicken or pork, and with Chinese crispy pork. Thai noodle salads also make a good match with Australian Marsanne.

Muscadet More generally known as Melon de Bourgogne, the Muscadet grape variety makes the acerbic, neutrally flavoured white wine of the western Loire that bears its name. Young and cold, it works well with spanking-fresh seafood (and will forgive the liberally applied mayonnaise you may like to douse it with), and with very plain grilled white fish. It's also handy for very highly spiced or oily ethnic dishes, such as pad thai (Thai noodles and beansprouts), Japanese tempura-battered prawns, Chinese squid fishcakes and Indian butter chicken. A **mature** Muscadet de Sèvre-et-Maine *sur lie* (with at least three years' bottle-age) will go productively with a range of cheeses, such as Chaource, Reblochon, Lancashire, and sheep's-milk Pecorino.

Muscat This grape, or family of grapes to be more precise (different strains of it are used in different wines), is as versatile with wine as its many styles would seem to promise. Vinified **dry** (as in the dry Muscats of Alsace), it goes well with certain fish dishes, including *sole véronique* and creamy-sauced salmon, as well as Thai-style stir-fried pork, Chinese kung pao chicken and Indian chicken Madras. **Late-picked**, it makes a crisply appetising match with a citrus-flavoured bavarois or mousse, and with chocolate brownies, frangipane-based fruit tarts and soufflés. The **fortified** Muscats of southern France (typified by Beaumes-de-Venise) go with many of the richest desserts, including most chocolate creations, hot banana dishes (toffee bananas and baked bananas), and sherry trifle. Australia's super-syrupy **Liqueur Muscats**, made in the Rutherglen region of Victoria, are good if you have used some of the wine itself in the dessert recipe (for example, to replace the rum in a baba, or else poured over vanilla or chocolate ice-cream).

Pinot Blanc This grape variety, best exemplified by Alsace Pinot Blanc, but also grown in northern Italy, Germany (where they call it Weissburgunder) and California, makes a good, neutral backdrop to almost any delicately flavoured white fish or poultry dish where it is important that the wine doesn't hog the limelight. Sashimi, couscous and vegetarian nut roasts are also good contexts for Pinot Blanc.

Pinot Gris One of the leading grapes of Alsace, also starring in Oregon, Germany (as Ruländer or Grauburgunder) and northern Italy (as Pinot Grigio), Pinot Gris can be rather neutral, but at its best – as in Alsace – has a spicy edge to it, as well as the kind of richness normally found in hot-climate Chardonnays. Stuffed peppers, chicken bhuna, Thai green chicken curry and stir-fried pork are all good with it, as are the lighter-fleshed game birds, skate served with a meat-stock sauce and mashed potato, trout with almonds, and starters such as warm onion tart.

Riesling Immensely versatile for its range of styles, and for its snappy, lime-scented sharpness, the best Riesling wines come from Germany, Alsace, Australia and New Zealand. **Dry** wines are good with chilli-hot Indian dishes such as chicken jalfrezi or Madras, and with the lime leaf and lemongrass seasonings of Thai food, particularly green curries. They also work with soft cheeses such as Boursin and most goats' cheeses. **Late-picked** wines are excellent with many light desserts, including strawberries and cream, crème caramel, plum crumble and profiteroles, and with the powerfully aromatic Alsace cheese, Munster. **Fully rotted** versions, such as the Sélection de Grains Nobles of Alsace, or botrytised wines from Australia or California, are brilliant with pancakes and maple syrup, or chocolate-sauced pear belle-Hélène.

Sauvignon Blanc Dry, tartly acidic and teeming with ripe fruit, Sauvignon makes highly appetising dry white wines, with the best coming from the upper Loire (Sancerre, Pouilly-Fumé and Menetou-Salon), South Africa, Hungary and New Zealand. Brilliant with goat's cheeses, asparagus, smoked eel, red mullet, smoked haddock, Indian king prawn rogan josh, Thai noodle salads and stir-fried squid, Japanese tempura-battered prawns, and ratatouille, it is useful wherever sharp seasonings and a certain amount of acidity in the food mandate a sharply textured wine. It is one of the few dry whites to be able to cope with salads dressed in lemony vinaigrette, and tomato doesn't frighten it either. It is also good with Cheshire and Lancashire cheeses, and Cornish Yarg.

Semillon Mostly blended with Sauvignon in the dry and sweet white wines of Bordeaux, or with Chardonnay in Australia, Semillon is also important as a dry varietal wine in Australia (especially in the Hunter Valley), and as a botrytised dessert wine. **Dry** wines are good with white crabmeat, monkfish, a classic British potato-topped fish pie, densely textured poultry such as turkey and guinea-fowl, India's vindaloo dishes, and Chinese sweetcorn soup. **Botrytised** Semillon, such as Sauternes and Barsac, is excellent with a multitude of the richest and creamiest desserts, such as crème brûlée, bread-and-butter pudding, tiramisu and *îles flottantes* (floating islands), and with certain salty blue cheeses, Roquefort pre-eminent among them. Some people like to drink Sauternes with foie gras.

Sylvaner One of the lesser grape varieties of Alsace, and of the Franken region of Germany, Sylvaner/Silvaner tends to have a distinctly vegetal edge, not dissimilar to cooked cabbage. Try it with grilled plaice, rice-stuffed peppers, Thai stir-fried squid, chicken, pork or rabbit dishes cooked with mustard, or Munster cheese.

Verdejo A grassy-flavoured grape of northern Spain, where it is important in the wines of Rueda, Verdejo goes well with lightly dressed salads, seafood, plain-grilled fish dishes, or a Spanish omelette or tortilla.

Verdelho This is one of the grape varieties of madeira, but is also important now as a weighty, citrus-flavoured dry varietal wine in Australia. Try it with grilled John Dory, Chinese crispy pork and lemon chicken, or the brightly spicy chicken dishes of Pacific Rim cooking with its southeast Asian influences.

Vernaccia An indigenous grape variety of central Italy, as in the Tuscan wine Vernaccia di San Gimignano, Vernaccia – and indeed many other very delicately fla-voured Italian dry whites – is best with deep-fried scampi and *fritto misto*, white fish (such as skate or sea bass) steamed in the Chinese style with spring onions and ginger, India's chicken dhansak, and mild cheeses such as Taleggio and Edam.

Viognier Once unknown outside the northern Rhône,

Viognier is now grown in the pays d'Oc, California, Australia and Chile. It makes a fat-textured wine with juicy peach or apricot fruit, bright lemony acidity and, in the best examples, an appetising note of aromatic spice. Thai red curries, sushi, vegetable terrine, Indian korma and even vindaloo dishes, creamy-sauced turbot, halibut, red mullet, brown crabmeat and cooked lobster are the kinds of foods to put alongside it.

Viura The principal white grape of Rioja makes some very appealing, **unoaked**, lemony dry wines on its own these days. In this style, it goes well with salmon fishcakes, red snapper, plain-grilled trout, pepper-stuffed Spanish tortillas, Chinese spring rolls, or India's onion bhajis and buttery makhani dishes. The **oaky** style of white Rioja Crianza or Reserva is best with strongly flavoured savoury dishes such as skate with brown butter, trout with almonds, stewed tuna, and strong cheeses such as Parmesan and Ireland's Milleens.

ROSÉ WINES
Still rosé wines go well with many fish dishes, especially salmon and pink-fleshed trout, and with baked ham, casseroled rabbit, cooked lobster dishes, ratatouille, paella, Japanese teriyaki, and hot Thai noodle dishes.

RED WINES
Aglianico A distinguished grape variety of southwest Italy, where it appears in an aromatic, robust red wine called Aglianico del Vulture, this is a good choice with Italian bolognese sauces, hearty slow-cooked lamb dishes such as Irish stew and Lancashire hotpot, with Japanese teriyaki, and with Parmesan.

Barbera This northern Italian grape variety from Piedmont, also grown in Argentina and California, is extremely versatile with food, matching tomato-based meat sauces, shepherd's pie, Cumberland sausages, lasagne, and meaty fish dishes such as monkfish wrapped in Parma ham. It also works with a variety of Italian cheeses, from Provolone to Gorgonzola.

Cabernet Franc One of the main three red grape varieties of Bordeaux, Cabernet Franc appears as a varietal in certain red wines of the central Loire, such as Chinon, Bourgueil, St-Nicolas-de-Bourgueil and Saumur-Champigny. These lightish, juicy-fruited reds go well with Thai-style chicken satay and beef in peanut sauce, traditional roast beef, baked ham, and a few cheeses, such as Brie, Cheshire and softer blues like Blue Vinney.

Cabernet Sauvignon Grown all over the viticultural world now, Cabernet Sauvignon (often seen in blends with Merlot, Cabernet Franc or Shiraz) has come to seem the pre-eminent red varietal wine. At its best when rich and rounded, and with concentrated flavours of ripe purple fruits, it is an enormously adaptable wine at the table. It will go with most red meats from quail to venison, via beef, lamb and duck, and is also good with the more firmly textured types of organ meat, such as calf's kidneys and lamb's liver. It has its uses with Indian cooking too, where red-hot Madras sauces don't in the least intimidate it. Among cheeses, Beaufort, Gruyère, mature Caerphilly and even Ireland's Cashel Blue go well with the riper, sweeter styles of Cabernet Sauvignon from Australia. Cabernet-based Bordeaux is one of the all-time classic matches with roast lamb.

Dolcetto Grown in northwest Italy's Piedmont region, Dolcetto makes delightfully light, juicy reds with the tang of ripe blueberries about them. Its wines are best suited to highly seasoned and fatty dishes such as Chinese crispy pork or duck with ginger and pineapple, Indian lamb biryani, grilled pork chops, herby sausages, steak tartare, cooked ox tongue, and of course classic Italian dishes such as beef-based lasagne and cannelloni. The lighter styles of blue cheese, such as Dolcelatte and Bleu de Bresse, are good with Dolcetto.

Gamay The Beaujolais grape makes light, strawberryish reds with high acidity but no tannin to speak of. Its wines are good with salmon or tuna, garlicky stuffed mushrooms, lamb samosas, a range of roasts from chicken and pork to beef, rabbit in mustard sauce, and calf's liver. Brie, Pont-l'Evêque and St-Nectaire are among its favoured cheese partners. It's also rather good as an accompaniment to unsweetenend red fruits, especially raspberries.

Grenache/Garnacha Important in the southern Rhône (e.g. Châteauneuf-du-Pape, Gigondas and Vacqueyras), in the Languedoc, in northern Spain and in Australia, Grenache tends to be blended with such other grapes as Syrah/Shiraz, Carignan and Mourvèdre. These Rhône-style or Spanish-style blends, as we can think of them, go well with roast birds such as duck and goose, as well as with most of the game birds from partridge to grouse, with roast beef and lamb, oxtail and calf's liver. They are excellent with highly spiced dishes – chilli con carne, Szechuan sizzling beef, Thai chicken satay and beef in peanut sauce – cheesy dishes such as cauliflower gratin, and earthy dishes like the vegetarian version of moussaka. Languedoc blends such as Corbières and Minervois are the traditional partners to cassoulet. Mature Cheddar, Double Gloucester, Gruyère and French Tomme are among the cheeses to serve with them.

Merlot Merlot predominates in the clarets of the Pomerol district of Bordeaux, and is vinified as a varietal just about everywhere else in the world, for its soft, plummy style of wine, suitable where the wine isn't required to exercise any bite on the food it is accompanying. It's good with tuna, with rich meats such as pigeon and quail, oxtail and kangaroo, densely textured white meats such as turkey (where it's wonderful with sage and onion stuffing) and guinea-fowl, simple everyday dishes such as cottage pie and goulash, and a host of traditional European meat dishes from cassoulet to moussaka. If you're looking to partner a cheese with it, think of the hard cow's-milk varieties such as Cheddar, Caerphilly and even Stilton.

Nebbiolo The grape of Barolo and Barbaresco in north-west Italy, Nebbiolo is renowned for producing towering, forbiddingly tannic reds of great toughness, but these days, many producers are aiming for a softer, more flexible feel. Pair it with such classic Italian dishes as tomato-sauced chicken wrapped in Parma ham, with meaty pasta sauces, pigeon, dark-fleshed game birds such as grouse and wood-cock, osso bucco, jugged hare, calf's liver, cauliflower gratin, and pungent, firm-textured cheeses such as Spanish Manchego.

Pinot Noir The lighter style of red epitomised by Pinot Noir is best found in Burgundy, California, Oregon and New Zealand. It works beautifully served slightly chilled with certain fish: grilled salmon and seared tuna, red snapper and hake. All kinds of chicken dishes go well with it, from simple roast chicken to chicken chasseur, barbe-cued and southern-fried chicken, and it is the classic accompaniment to coq au vin. A mature Pinot comes into its own with well-hung game birds such as grouse and partridge. It's great with everyday dishes too, though, such as corned beef hash and meatloaf, and with organ meats like kidneys. The less highly spiced of ethnic dishes suit it well (try lamb rogan josh or Japanese teriyaki), as do vegetarian dishes based on mushrooms. Soft cow's-milk cheeses are its best friends on the cheeseboard, with the French ones such as Brie, Camembert and Epoisses show-ing particularly well. As an unusual treat, a glass of chilled Pinot Noir is a fine partner for a bowl of ripe red summer fruits, either strawberries or raspberries.

Sangiovese The principal grape of Tuscany in central Italy, also grown in Argentina and California, Sangiovese is a surefire bet with tomatoey Italian dishes. Any tomato-based pasta sauce and most pizzas are great with Chianti Classico, or any of the other Sangiovese-based blends. These wines are also good with roast quail, roast pork, shepherd's pie, melanzane alla parmigiana, and cheeses such as Pont l'Evêque and Gouda, where either the lightness or the acidity in the wines helps to fashion a precise gastronomic marriage.

Shiraz/Syrah Made as a varietal wine in the northern Rhône (Hermitage, Crozes-Hermitage, St-Joseph, Côte-Rôtie and Cornas), and also in Australia, South Africa, California and Chile, Shiraz/Syrah is a perfect choice with spicy, especially peppery, dishes. It is unimpeachable with steak au poivre, but is often surprisingly good with apparently gentler foods, such as roast turkey, goose, rabbit and well-hung game birds. Beef bourguignonne, venison, oxtail, beef sausages, merguez sausages, and chilli con carne are all good with this grape, and among the ethnic dishes, shami kebab, Szechuan beef and teri-yaki dishes all work well. Among cheeses, the best matches are with Swiss Appenzell, French Tomme and mature Cheshire.

Tempranillo Spain's Number One red grape is the mainstay of Rioja and Navarra reds, Ribera del Duero and Valdepeñas, and crops up in a host of lesser wines too. Its very best food partners are roast poultry and roast lamb, with which it makes quite as traditional a pairing as claret. It's good with homely dishes such as cottage pie, sausages and mash, barbecued chicken wings, tripe in a Spanish-style tomatoey stew, and spicy kebabs. With stuffed peppers or a tortilla, it makes a comfortingly gentle match, and a mature Rioja Reserva is a delight with the Spanish sheep's-milk cheese Manchego, and also with Irish Milleens.

Zinfandel The best versions of Californian Zinfandel are rich and rounded reds, full of juicy brambly fruit, with a distinct note of spicy sweetness on the finish. These wines are excellent with fruity-sauced duck (especially black cherries), barbecued steaks, burgers, blackened Cajun-style chicken, fillet steak with black pepper sauce, chorizo sausage, venison, calf's liver, Chinese beef in black bean sauce and duck with ginger and pineapple, and Japanese teriyaki dishes. Hard cheeses with a slightly sweet edge to them, such as France's Comté, are a good choice with Zinfandel, which also makes an appealing match with mature Stilton.

FORTIFIED WINES

Fortified and Liqueur Muscats See Muscat under White Wines, earlier in this chapter.

Madeira The drier versions of madeira, **Sercial and Verdelho**, are excellent with cheeses such as mature Cheshire and Caerphilly, while the richer and sweeter styles, **Bual and Malmsey**, are brilliant with Stilton, and also with rich dark fruitcake.

Marsala Drink the best type, marsala dolce, with those desserts that also contain it, such as tiramisu and zabaglione. It's also good with toffee-flavoured desserts, such as toffee cheesecake and pecan pie, and isn't bad with a piece of old Parmesan or Grana Padano cheese.

Port Basic **ruby** port is good with mature Cheddar and other similar hard cow's-milk cheeses. Trade up to an **LBV** (late-bottled vintage), and the choice becomes wider, even encompassing the odd blue such as Scottish Dunsyre. Port and Stilton is much liked by many, but **tawny** port is more of a winner with Stilton than ruby, and also goes well with Dunsyre. **White** port makes an appealing partner for Chinese sweet-and-sour dishes.

Sherry The driest styles of sherry, **fino** and **manzanilla**, are excellent aperitifs, and also go superbly well with olives and most tapas dishes, as well as with Thailand's chilli-hot tom yum soup, Japanese miso soup and that Chinese takeaway favourite, chicken and cashew nuts. Baked sea bream is a fine main-course dish to match it with. Try it too with ripe Reblochon cheese. A medium-sweet **amontillado** is good with firmly textured blue cheeses and with sherry trifle (assuming you've used some in the dish), while the very sweetest and richest **olorosos** are best with very mature Cheddar and Parmesan, or pecan pie. The unloved style of **pale cream** sherry is a winner with Chinese lemon chicken, and with English rice pudding. Pour the thickly raisiny **PX** (Pedro Ximénez) sherry over vanilla ice-cream.

GLOSSARY

Age/Ageing Refers to the capability of a wine to improve with keeping. Wines might 'age' in oak barrels in the producer's cellars; similarly, they may be aged in the bottle at home by the buyer. Not every wine has the capacity to age. Many white wines, and a few reds, are intended to be drunk while as young and as fresh as possible (usually before the wines of the following vintage are released). Most red wines, and a few whites such as Chablis and other burgundies, and German Rieslings, benefit from a period of keeping. This can be anything from a few months for a dry white wine, to many years in the case of the richest reds.

Blanc de blancs In champagne, denotes the style of wine made entirely from the region's sole white grape, Chardonnay. Usually lighter in texture than others, but can go progressively deeper and richer with age.

Blanc de noirs Champagne term used for wines made entirely from one or both of the two permitted black grape varieties of the region, Pinot Noir and Pinot Meunier.

Blended Used mainly in this book to denote wines made of two or more grape varieties. The opposite of a varietal (qv).

Blush Term for still, pink wines widely used in the

United States, and to a lesser degree in other English-speaking wine countries.

Botrytised Describes sweet wine made from grapes that have been attacked by the fungus *Botrytis cinerea*, known in English as 'noble rot', to distinguish it from the ignoble kinds that only ruin the grapes. Botrytis shrivels the grapes on the vine, drying out their water content, but concentrating the natural sugars in the fruit. Botrytised wines are wholly natural sweet wines, therefore, in that they haven't had any extraneous sweetening element added to them. In Europe, traditional botrytised wines are not indicated as such on the label. You are simply expected to know that this is the style of wine that comes out of a bottle labelled 'Sauternes'. However, in the so-called New World countries, the wine name generally does give the relevant information (e.g. 'Botrytised Riesling').

Bottle-age Denotes the length of time a wine has been in the bottle. Many wines are aged for a period in the cellars of the winemaker, so the bottle-age isn't necessarily counted from the year of the vintage, but when the notes speak of a wine with 'a couple of years' bottle-age', the couple of years can safely be counted from the year on the label.

Brut Of sparkling wine, very dry. The most popular style.

Cask age The length of time a wine has been matured in barrels by the winemaker. Generally stated on the back label, although some producers of classic French wines still bottle their wines without back-labels, in the interests, presumably, of creating a secret-recipe mystique around the wine.

Classed growth See under 'Cru'.

Crianza Spanish term that indicates a wine that has been subjected to a legally defined minimum ageing period in oak barrels before release, generally one year for reds and six months for whites.

Cru Literally 'growth'. Used to denote particular vineyard land that has been legally designated as being of notably superior quality (see also 'premier cru' and 'grand cru'). A cru Beaujolais comes from any one of ten specifically named vineyard areas within the region, as opposed to the basic stuff, which is Beaujolais or Beaujolais-Villages. In Bordeaux, the wine classification system operated in certain districts ranks the wines into hierarchically organised quality categories known as *crus classés*, or classed growths.

Demi-sec Medium-dry. Not a sweet wine, but one that has a noticeable quotient of residual sugar in it. Sometimes defined in English as 'off-dry'.

Finish The impression left by a wine in the mouth once it has been swallowed. The finish is composed partly of flavour attributes, but also the length of time the aftertaste persists on the palate. A wine with 'a good finish' lingers on for anything up to a minute.

Fortified wine One that has had grape spirit added to it, increasing the alcohol level above that of table wine. Classic types are sherry, port, madeira and marsala, but many are being made outside Europe now too.

Grand cru The highest quality designation within Burgundy, Alsace, Champagne and the wines of the St-Emilion district (though not the other districts) of Bordeaux. Refers to specifically defined vineyard land, rather than anything about the winemaking process.

Moelleux Sweet. The sweetest style, for example, of the Loire Valley wine Vouvray, but not generally quite as sweet as wines affected by botrytis (see 'botrytised').

Oaked/Oaky Wines that have been matured in oak barrels, in some cases also having undergone their initial fermentation in the barrel as well. This information will generally be presented on the back label (or may, in a few cases, have been worked into the name of the wine itself, as in 'Barrel-Fermented Chardonnay'), but note that in many of the classic wine areas of old Europe, such as France, Spain, Italy and Portugal, there may be no back label on the bottle, and no information on the front either. Some producers, intent on making a cost-effective wine with the flavour of oak, resort to one of the permitted short cuts, such as dunking oak chips in a stainless steel vat of wine.

Off-dry See 'demi-sec'.

Premier cru Literally 'first growth'. It designates particular patches of vineyard land that are considered to be above the average within a wine district, but confusingly, it is lower in Burgundy's and Champagne's quality hierarchies than 'grand cru' (qv). So, in descending order of illustriousness, it's Chablis grand cru, Chablis premier cru, Chablis. In the Médoc and Graves districts of Bordeaux, on the other hand, premier cru is the top.

Reserve/Réserve/Reserva/Riserva Respectively English, French, Spanish and Italian terms used, often without the full panoply of legal force, to denote wines that are a cut above the norm, either because they come from plots of land that the proprietor considers his better vineyards, or because they have been aged a bit longer before release. For Spanish wines, Reserva does indicate that the wine has been given a certain legally required minimum maturation period in oak, generally twelve months for reds, six for whites. The designation is one step up from 'crianza' (qv) because the *overall* ageing process, which may be completed in the bottle, is longer. Italian wines may also be subject to legally specified maturation periods, but these may be in barrel or bottle, and the periods vary from one denominated wine to the next.

Rotted Made from grapes affected by noble rot (see 'botrytised').

Rounded out Refers to a wine that has achieved a state of maturity, in which its youthful tannins and/or acidity have softened, resulting in a smoother feel in the mouth.

Sur lie Term seen on the better grades of Muscadet, indicating that the wine has been kept for a while on its post-fermentation yeast sediments, lending a softer texture to it.

Tannin The naturally occurring substance in the skins of grapes that contributes to the rough or astringent feeling in the mouth imparted by young red wines. It derives from the fact that the juice of red grapes must be vinified in contact with the grapeskins in order to give it colour. Most red wines will lose their tannin as they age in the bottle, although a few do not. Tannin is also present in wood, and so the tannin level of a red wine may be jointly derived from the grapeskins and the barrels the wine was matured in.

Unoaked Refers to wines that have had no contact at all with oak during their production. Generally used of white wines, and often touted now as a particular selling-point in those wines (e.g. Australian Chardonnay) that have traditionally been thought of as oaky wines.

Varietal The name for a wine produced from one single grape variety. The opposite of a blend.

Varietal labelling The practice of naming the wine after its grape variety or blend of varieties. A revolution brought about by producers in the non-European wine countries, it hasn't penetrated Europe to as great a degree because the wine laws there specify that wines should be given geographical names (after the region, village or even particular vineyard plot they were grown in).

Vintage With certain wines, pre-eminently champagne and port, the term 'vintage' implies a wine of higher quality produced from a single year's harvest. These are wines that are only produced in the good years, when a hot growing season has ripened the grapes to perfection, and there was no rain during the harvest time. In Champagne, for example, 1990 was a vintage year, but 1994 was not. Grapes harvested in the latter year would therefore go into a non-vintage blend. In the main, though, with table wines that are produced every year, no matter what the growing conditions, the vintage simply refers to the year itself, so that one talks of a wine 'from the 2002 vintage', without implying that 2002 is in any way special.

INDEX